Advice for Beginning Teachers

Educators' Letters to Their Younger Selves

Sara Coble Simmons

Advice for Beginning Teachers

Educators' Letters to Their Younger Selves

Kendall Hunt
publishing company

Cover image © Shutterstock.com

Kendall Hunt
publishing company

www.kendallhunt.com
Send all inquiries to:
4050 Westmark Drive
Dubuque, IA 52004-1840

Copyright © 2017 by Sara Coble Simmons

ISBN 978-1-5249-2258-0

Published in the United States of America

Teaching is the essential profession, the one that makes all other professions possible

*Attributed to David Haselkorn, President of the non-profit group, Recruiting New Teachers, Inc., 1996; included in **Promising Practices: New Ways to Improve Teacher Quality** (1998), a U.S. Department of Education report that evolved from the President's Summit on Teacher Quality.*

TABLE OF CONTENTS

PREFACE

The writers whose letters have been selected to be included in this edited collection are individuals from a wide range of backgrounds and experiences, from aspiring teachers who are looking forward to launching their careers, to veteran educators who have served in a variety of roles over many years. The letters are a vehicle through which they provide advice and counsel to the novice teachers that they soon will be, or that they once were. Their letters address what they judge to be most critical issues facing a new teacher and offer suggestions for handling these in ways that allow them to be true to the core values and beliefs they hold most dear. Their words of wisdom ring true because they are written from deep within the hearts of these outstanding educators who *have changed*— or, in the case of the aspiring teachers, soon *will change*—countless lives.

This book celebrates those who have chosen teaching, the most noble of professions, and pays tribute to their commitment and dedication to making a positive difference in the lives of our children. It is hoped that these voices of wisdom and experience will uplift, inspire, affirm, encourage, reassure, empower, entertain, and, at times, tug at the reader's heart strings and, perhaps, elicit empathic tears.

The intended audience for this book is a broad range of people involved and interested in education and in educators. Pre-service and novice teachers, who are just beginning their careers in this challenging but rewarding profession, are an especially appropriate audience. In these letters, they will find a wealth of reliable advice and practical suggestions that are worthy of taking to heart. Other intended audiences include professors who train new teachers, veteran teachers who mentor them, and administrators who supervise them. From reading the letters, those individuals who are blessed to be able to work with aspiring or beginning teachers will be able to glean ideas for providing guidance during those critical early years of teaching. Each of these groups will benefit from the insights contained in the letters. Undoubtedly, this book should appeal to a wide range of readers—whether they have zero years of experience, are long retired, or fit somewhere in between.

Readers will find that each letter is unique in voice, style, and substance, and each provides its own distinctive view into the awesome, but challenging, world that a beginning teacher enters. Each letter is filled with sage advice to help the neophyte teacher to not only *survive* the first year, but also to *thrive* over the years to follow as a leader in the classroom and in the school, and to find success and meaning in a demanding profession in an ever-changing society.

In the current context of education in our nation, words of sound advice and stirring inspiration are especially needed by our pre-service teachers and beginning teachers. I feel honored and privileged to have been able to compile this incredible collection of letters!

Sara Coble Simmons

June 15, 2017

ACKNOWLEDGEMENTS AND DEDICATION

The letters in this collection were written by a diverse group of educators—both aspiring teachers and seasoned professionals—who wrote to their future, first-year teacher selves, or to their younger, less experienced selves. I applaud the pre-service teachers for looking into the future and providing thought-provoking guidance to themselves as rookie teachers. By doing so, they reinforced in their own minds the most desirable attributes of the teachers they want to become. Similarly, I sincerely appreciate the willingness of the veteran educators to take a trip down memory lane to recall how they felt as fledgling teachers and to remember what all they DIDN'T know at that time. They took on the challenge of composing a letter to their younger, less experienced selves, in order to offer enlightenment about what is most important to fret over, and what is not.

Invariably, the writers have expressed that they found this experience of composing their letters to be deeply rewarding. They are optimistic that their advice, if heeded, can help those who are new to this profession to focus on the crucial keys to success, so that they not only *persevere and overcome* the challenges of their first year, but also *prevail and flourish* in the years to come.

The aspiring teachers and veteran educators whose letters are included in this book have given permission for their letters to be published. These letters are in the original words of the writers, except for relatively minor changes, such as a few words added here and there for clarification or other minor edits.

If the writers included the names of specific public schools, colleges/ universities, agencies, and/or people in their letters, these generally have been removed in order to minimize distractions and, instead, to focus the reader's attention on the deeper insights contained in the letters. Letter writers' suggestions of books, articles, and other resources for new teachers to read have been retained, and a list of references have been included at the end of letters, as applicable.

An index lists the names of the 50 contributors who submitted letters. They each have my utmost respect and admiration. They cared enough to share their hard-won wisdom with the readers of this book. To those readers, I humbly dedicate this work.

ABOUT THE AUTHOR/EDITOR

Dr. Sara Coble Simmons has spent over 40 years in various facets of public education in three different states—North Carolina, Virginia, and Texas. She earned her BA in Elementary Education and MEd in Guidance and Counseling from The University of North Carolina at Greensboro and her PhD in Curriculum and Instruction from The University of Texas at Austin. She was a public school teacher for 20 years and has worked at the Texas Education Agency and as an independent educational consultant. In July 2017, she retired as a full professor in the School of Education at The University of North Carolina at Pembroke.

While at UNC Pembroke, Dr. Simmons taught 29 different professional core courses for undergraduate and graduate education programs. She received the University's Outstanding Teaching Award in 2005 and 2016, both times after being nominated by students. She was nominated for the prestigious North Carolina Board of Governors' Award for Excellence in Teaching in fall 2016. She was the Associate Dean of the School of Education from 2007 to 2008, and Dean of the School of Graduate Studies from 2008 to 2012. She was elected by her faculty peers to serve as the Chair of the General Faculty, Chair of the Faculty Senate, and Chair of the Faculty Senate Executive Committee from 2016 to 2017.

Dr. Simmons is the founding President of the North Carolina Association of Elementary Educators (NCAEE) and has served on its board of directors and on numerous standing committees. She also has been active in the North Carolina Association of Colleges and Teacher Educators (NC-ACTE), having served on the Executive Committee and as Co-Chair and Chair of the association's Annual North Carolina Teacher Education Forum. She has directed various grant-funded collaborative projects to support teachers—especially beginning teachers—in area public schools. Her areas of research interest include standards-aligned instructional design, differentiated instruction, classroom assessment, online pedagogy, and teacher mentoring and induction. She consults with school districts and schools and has given well over a hundred peer-reviewed presentations at varied state, national, and international professional conferences. Along with two colleagues, she is the author of the textbook, *Discovering the Teacher Within You: An Introduction to Education in North Carolina*, published in 2016 by Kendall Hunt Publishing Company. She strives to stay current on state and national educational issues, and she enjoys meeting people and engaging in a lively exchange of ideas about teaching and learning and educational improvement.

Dr. Simmons may be contacted via email (scsimmons@windstream.net or sara.simmons@uncp.edu) or through the publisher, Kendall Hunt Publishing Company (https://www.kendallhunt.com/ or https://www.kendallhunt.com/corporate/contact).

INTRODUCTION

"Who dares to teach must never cease to learn."

John Cotton Dana (1856–1929), American librarian and museum director, composed for inscription on a new building at Newark State College (now Kean College of New Jersey), Union, New Jersey.

Teaching and learning are inseparable. Of course, educators teach others, but they themselves also learn compelling lessons from their daily interactions with children, parents and families, and colleagues. Too often, educators' hard-won wisdom, acquired over time, is left unarticulated and unspoken. The harried, hurried, and stressful lives of today's school teachers and administrators leave little time to engage in written reflection on the insights gained from their day-to-day practice.

Based on the belief that these voices of experience need and deserve to be heard, this book project was initiated so that this accumulation of wisdom would be elicited and preserved. Individuals in a variety of educational roles (e.g., aspiring teachers, practicing teachers, instructional coaches, mentors, administrators, central office personnel, university professors) were invited to participate in this exciting project. They were asked to write a letter to their first-year-teacher self, which required them to examine important influences that have shaped them, both as individuals and as prospective or current professional educators.

In composing their letters to themselves as beginning teachers, these writers have had an opportunity to reflect on their uniquely personal experiences and to clarify their views about what constitutes "good" teaching. For the pre-service teachers, writing their letters caused them to envision themselves in the future and to think deeply about the kind of teacher they want to become. By recalling an earlier period in their lives, those who are experienced practitioners were prompted to recall with greater clarity how they themselves have changed with time. In their letters, these seasoned educators have addressed what they believe to be the most pressing issues a novice teacher is facing and offer advice for handling these issues in ways that are aligned with their deeply held values and beliefs.

This book is a compilation of best of those letters, which shed light on what these writers believe to be "fundamental truths" about teaching and learning and reflect a clear and coherent philosophy of education. The initial section includes letters written by pre-service teachers to impart advice to their future selves to prepare them for their first year of teaching. The other letters are presented in chapters that are organized according to the teaching assignments of the teachers for their initial year (e.g., early childhood and elementary, middle and secondary, specialty areas).

If you are an aspiring teacher or a first-year teacher, the letters included in this book will provide valuable insights and practical advice and will invite you to find the humor in your day-to-day work with children. If successful, this book will inspire and motivate you to persevere in your chosen profession. If you are an educator with more years of accumulated experience, you will be prompted to relive your own poignant journey down the path to greater enlightenment and to recall the myriad ways in which you acquired your "wisdom of practice." Whether you are an educator or not, you may be stimulated to recall the teachers you had as you progressed through school and to reflect on how those teachers' values and beliefs were revealed in their practice and how that influenced you as a learner.

> **This book celebrates all who have chosen this most noble of professions and pays tribute to their future selves, who continue to dedicate themselves to making a difference in the lives of our children—one day at a time, one child at a time.**

Advice for Beginning Teachers

Educators' Letters to Their Younger Selves

Letters Written by Aspiring Educators to their Future Selves

(authored by individuals who are not yet "officially" hired as teachers)

"I do not think much of a man who is not wiser today than he was yesterday."

Abraham Lincoln (1809–1865), American lawyer and legislator, 16th U.S. President, 1861–1865

Dear excited first-year April,

Oh my goodness! Look at you, getting ready for your very first class. You are definitely excited, energetic, and dressed to impress… for now, anyways. You have graduated from school, you have observed in classrooms, and you have even completed a semester of student teaching, but remember, that is merely a scrape on the surface. So you are ready, right? WRONG! You will never be ready, but that's okay. Just bear with me as I give you some tips.

The first piece of advice I will give you, is *time management*. Your first year you are going to have so many new teacher meetings, and you will be learning the grading system and getting to know your peers, but just relax. You will be tired, but you will also learn to roll with the tide. Take time to write things down and prioritize. Also, don't forget about those two lovely boys you have at home. They won't help you with grading your students' work, but they sure will be there to make you smile. Things are going to get crazy, but don't become over-whelmed. If you need help, ask for it!

My second piece of advice is that *you are not perfect and you will mess up a few times*. Yes, I know this is way out of character for you, but it's going to happen. You missed an after-school meeting because you had to pick up your sons from their grandma's. Will you get a warning? Probably, but it is okay. Just make sure you let your principal know it was a mistake and move on. Will you enter a grade wrong and a parent will call and complain? Yes, but it is okay. If you're going to cry, wait until you get home. You are going to make mistakes, but keep your head. You will do way more good than bad.

My third piece of advice is that *even though it is cute, doesn't mean it will work*. This includes your classroom décor and your dress. You know all those cute colorful bins, folders, and binders that you think will keep you and your students organized? They won't, but you will find something that works for you and your students, and it will change every year. Oh yes, let's not forget that cute long-sleeve cardigan you are ready to wear in the winter. The seasons are opposite inside your classroom. In the winter, it will be hot, and in the summer it will be cold, but it is ok, you will adjust. Also, those high-heel shoes you have, throw them out! They give you nothing but heartache, not to mention aching feet!

My fourth piece of advice is that *everything doesn't go the way it is planned*. No two days will ever be the same. Monday will go as planned and be absolutely wonderful, but Tuesday will be horrible. Timmy had an allergic reaction, and Sarah tripped and broke her glasses. With that being said, you also need to make sure you know which students have allergies and keep their medicine handy. Anyways, like I was saying, your days will be different, but don't compare them to the day before. Be FLEXIBLE. If you aren't flexible now, you better get to learning how!

Most importantly, *trust yourself*! Yes, you are a new teacher, but you were also a new mother at one time. You will learn as you go and change things accordingly. Be confident because students smell fear. You will be successful, and remember to always appreciate the small things.

Also remember, *being a teacher will be the most demanding, challenging thing you will ever do*. It will push you to your absolute max. It will almost break you. There will be times when it will feel like life has kicked you right in the stomach. However, teaching will also be the most beautiful thing that has ever happened to you. Weird, right? Believe me I know, but trust me. This is a giving profession, so give all you got. You are important! You are here for the students. To uplift them, to encourage them, to love them. You will carry out so many roles in your classroom that will go unrecognized by most, but not by those students.

Just remember to speak kindly, but firm, and stand tall and don't buckle. Be a leader, but always listen. Know what you are teaching, and if you have questions, ask! Also, be very observant and giving. Make your students laugh, because this may be the only place they ever feel joy, and never forget that to teach is to learn continuously, and when that dies, then you have nothing left.

Now, I wish you all the luck as you enter this wonderful profession. Learn from your mistakes and know that you can't help everyone. Be strong and believe in yourself. *Way to go new teacher!!!*

Forever grateful,
April Maynor

Dear Speaker of the Trees,

Congratulations! Today is your day. You're off to great places! You're off and away!

—Dr. Seuss, *Oh, the Places You'll Go!* (Seuss, 1990)

You have worked so hard toward your goals and here you are, about to begin your first year of teaching. I know you have been anticipating this moment for quite some time and I would like to begin by saying, "YOU MADE IT!" I am so proud of you and all of your accomplishments you had made as an undergraduate student, and I am even more proud of the person you have become during your graduate school experience. You are a creative, intelligent, and talented individual, and I am excited to see what your first year of teaching will have in store for you. I have all the confidence in the world that you will be successful, but please take the following advice into consideration during your first year of teaching, and every succeeding year.

The more that you READ, the more things you will KNOW. The more that you LEARN, the more places you'll GO.

—Dr. Seuss, *I Can Read with My Eyes Shut* (Goodreads, 2016)

As you already know from your experience as a tutor at the university's writing center and as the department tutor of the biology department, education and experience go hand-in-hand. As the students will be learning from you, you will have plenty to learn from your students as well. The first year of teaching is perhaps the most crucial part of your teaching experience; there is so much to learn! Be sure to treat every experience of your first year of teaching as a learning experience.

As a first-year teacher, there will be tons of curve-balls thrown your way; therefore, it is important for you to get to know your students and their parents. It is common that first-year teachers are seen as "fresh meat" and are often treated as such. Be sure to reach out to fellow faculty and staff members for assistance during your first year, and also reach out to your students. It is important to have some sort of "support team" in place, especially during your first year. I know you just graduated with your "Masters of Arts in Teaching, Science Education, Specialization, grades 9 through 12" degree and you feel like you know everything you need to know, but in fact, you don't know as much as you think you do.

> *We've got to make noises in greater amounts! So, open your mouth, lad! For every voice counts!*
>
> —Dr. Seuss, *Horton Hears a Who!* (Early Moments, 2016)

I know veteran teachers can seem intimidating at first, but please remember to stay true to yourself and believe in yourself! It is okay to ask for help and guidance along the way, but don't rely on other faculty and staff members as your crutch. Instead of relying on other teachers to lead the way of your first year of teaching, collaborate with them by exchanging ideas, receiving opinions, and being there for each other for moral support. Believe it or not, there are things that you know that other teachers may not know, and vice versa.

> *Unless someone like you cares a whole awful lot, nothing is going to get better. It's not.*
>
> —Dr. Seuss, *The Lorax* (Goodreads, 2016)

As you begin teaching, it is important to get to know your students. I know that you will have no problem with doing so because your heart, mind, and soul have been exhibited through your hard work and dedication to your future students thus far. I am so proud of your developed abilities to communicate with others, collaborate with individuals and groups, as well as provide assistance for those in need. Seven years ago while you were in high school, I would have never perceived you as being as outgoing and caring as you are today. Through your experience working with the diversity office at your university, as well as tutoring people of different abilities, ethnicities, and backgrounds, you have exhibited the ability to accept others as who they are; you have freed yourself from bias.

I know this is a large fear of yours, but I assure you with patience, brevity, and confidence, you will succeed. I know it concerns you when you think about being approached by an angry parent, but as long as you have evidence and justification, you will do just fine. As you begin teaching, be sure to take notes about everything. This includes self-feedback on assessment methods, lesson plans, and your actions. Please be sure to keep a file for every student and to keep a record of their behavior, assessment, and performance. I assure you, if you do so, you will succeed as a first-year teacher.

> *Today you are you, that is truer than true. There is no one you-er than you.*
>
> —Dr. Seuss, *HAPPY BIRTHDAY TO YOU!* (Brightdrops, 2014)

I know that your first year of teaching is going to be hard. I know that you will have those days where you will say, "What have I done?", but I can assure you with patience, time, and dedication, you will become an excellent teacher. You have exhibited the capabilities of leadership, collaboration, and dedication through your past experiences as the president of our university's biology club and as a graduate assistant. I encourage you to take these abilities and add on to them by learning from others, and most of all, by learning from your students. I have heard you recite time and time again, *"My students are my reason, my students are my purpose,"* and I believe those are great words to live by, especially during your first year of teaching.

Please remember, although your students are of high importance, you are important as well. I know you have struggled in the past with self-confidence and setting time aside for yourself, but just as one of our guest speakers for our graduate class said, "confidence is key". Be sure to continue to attend workshops and conferences and add on to your professional development. Also, be sure to take time for yourself and ENJOY your first year teaching. Please do not worry too much and lose faith in yourself. I assure you, as long as you take my advice, you will succeed.

If you were never born, well then what would you do?

If you'd never been born, then what would you be?

You might be a fish! Or a toad in a tree!

You might be a doorknob!

Or three baked potatoes!

You might be a bag full of hard green tomatoes!

Or worse than that...Why, you might be a WASN'T!

A Wasn't has no fun at all.

No, he doesn't.

A Wasn't just isn't. He just isn't present.

But you...you are YOU!

And, now isn't that pleasant!

—Dr. Seuss, *HAPPY BIRTHDAY TO YOU* (Early Moments, 2016)

With faith, love, and wisdom to come, I will love you always.

The Speaker of the Trees
(Ashley Allen)

References

Brightdrops. (2014). 37 Dr. Seuss quotes that can change the world. Retrieved from http://brightdrops.com/dr-seuss-quotes

Early Moments. (2016). Favorite Dr. Seuss quotes. Retrieved from https://www.earlymoments.com/dr-seuss/Favorite-Dr-Seuss-Quotes/

Goodreads. (2016). I can read with my eyes shut! Quotes. Retrieved from https://www.goodreads.com/work/quotes/2333951-i-can-read-with-my-eyes-shut

Goodreads. (2016). The Lorax quotes. Retrieved from https://www.goodreads.com/work/quotes/886002-the-lorax

Seuss, Dr. (1990). *Oh the places you will go*. New York: Random House.

Dear Mr. Inspiration,

As you prepare to transition from the Soldier way of life to the Educator way of life, know that the values, traits, and competencies that made you successful as a Soldier will make you successful as an Educator. You have trained and prepared Soldiers for combat, but this differs from training and preparing students for life after high school. Let this letter be your guide and framework for your new journey.

First, remember that high school students are not Soldiers. You cannot use the same techniques and methods for instruction that you used in the military. You can and should hold the students to high standards, but you cannot demand it from them as if you are their drill sergeant. You must inspire them. This means you must get to know them. How you might ask? Observe, interact, and most importantly listen. Children do not have to be vocal for you to get to know them, but it will help. The more they feel that you genuinely care for them and their education, the more they will be willing to let you in and be receptive to what you can offer and teach them.

Second, use the experience around you. Most of the other teachers will be younger than you are, but they are the subject matter experts here. Don't forget what made you successful as a young Soldier. Pay attention to the good and the bad that is displayed from other teachers. Get to know them and find out what techniques they have had success and failure with. This is a new beginning for you, so treat it as such. Not that your service to your country isn't admired, but do not expect special treatment for serving, and do not expect the other teachers to immediately look up to you. You must earn the respect and confidence from your teacher colleagues with your actions, just as you had to do in the military.

Third, be more than just a teacher. Get involved with the school and the community. Provide help wherever necessary. You did not retire from the military and step into teaching to take a break. The school that you are working for needs more from you than just delivering lessons in the classroom. Coach a sport, lead a club, pick up whatever additional duty is required to make your school successful. Bring a new optic to old problems and develop innovative ideas to improve the situation. Be motivated! You already know from your time in the foxhole that optimism is a force multiplier.

Fourth, be patient. You have waited a long time for this, and I know that you want to change the world with your first class, but recognize that you need some development and polish before you can do that. Patience will be required when you encounter the occasional seasoned teacher or administrator that doesn't have that new fire that you have. Patience will be required when you encounter those students or fellow teachers that don't care what you did for the last 25 years. Patience will be required when disgruntled parents blame you for their child's failure or limited success and fail to see all the effort you have put in. Your students deserve your patience. Patience will be required if you are going to be a successful teacher.

Fifth, leadership is required on the battlefield and in the classroom. Setting the example in everything you do is critical to success. The students will be observing you in every way. They will observe your mannerisms, your attire, your cultural awareness, and your interactions with other students and teachers. Although you might think they are looking for flaws, they are looking for inspiration! You bring a lot of experience to the table, so find a way to use it. Don't force your experience on your students or coworkers. Let your actions inspire them to want to know more about who you are and what makes you tick. Let your actions inspire a fellow teacher who has lost her or his passion to reignite the flame that he or she once had. Let your actions influence students to apply 100% to not just their school work, but to every aspect of their lives. Inspire them to be better teenagers, citizens, and Americans. Inspire your students to work hard for their dreams. Above all, inspire your students to believe in themselves. Changing the world starts with inspiration.

Finally, have fun. You have the greatest job in the world. You are a high school teacher in the United States of America. You get to make a direct impact on the future generations of this great country. Their parents, and most importantly, the students themselves, are looking to you to guide them and put them on the right path. The enjoyment will not come from delivering an awesome lesson. Instead, it will come from watching your students grow from young boys and girls into young men and women who understand that they can be whatever they want and that they absolutely play a role in the future of humankind. Understand and accept that you may not reach every child, but never let that reality stop you from trying. Have fun. Enjoy every minute of it, because just as your first career has gone by too fast, so will this one. Good Luck!

Sincerely
Steven R. Abernathy

Greetings New Teacher John Ford,

Apparently you've successfully completed your graduate educator preparation program, and you are ready to commence your teaching career. Congratulations! Now that school is over, the real learning is about to begin. Pay attention.

You wanted to be a teacher in order to do meaningful work and make a contribution to the community. Perhaps you were impelled by noble impulses. You may have felt that you wanted to help educate young people so that they may become the future leaders of our country or have a greater chance to build good lives. Don't be disappointed if, when you get to your first assignment, you feel as if some of your fellow teachers seem somewhat less than idealistic and community-minded than you think they should be. In fact, some of them might even seem somewhat disaffected by their jobs! Teaching is difficult work, and some experienced teachers grouse a little bit. Remember, these experienced educators have probably been doing their jobs successfully for a long time, so reserve your judgement until you have been at your school for a while and have achieved some success of your own. And, if you hope to be at your new school for a while, it is a good idea to pay attention to the advice from your fellow teachers. They will be an invaluable resource. After all, they are the subject matter experts you'll come to depend on, and they know what is happening, especially what is happening within the local community.

Well, New Teacher, this isn't your first job. You are part of a bigger organization, and just like working in a restaurant, a newspaper, or the military, you'll be expected to represent the organization. At school, you'll be working under the guidance of a principal, following policies, working with fellow educators, teaching students, communicating with their parents, and functioning within the framework of a large school system. Be humble, be enthusiastic and be committed to the mission. Be professional. Support fellow teachers. Cooperate with the custodians, bus drivers, coaches, secretaries, counselors, lunch room staff, and all of the other valuable professionals who maintain the school infrastructure. Schools can't function without them.

Be the best teacher you can be. Be committed and worry about what you are doing instead of what others are doing. You'll have plenty to keep yourself busy. Work well with others, and don't participate in gossip, office politics, or any unethical behaviors.

Planning is something that will keep you busy, especially if you do it right. Because a failure to plan will produce embarrassing results, you'll have to research, seek advice, and conduct the best planning possible before the pedagogy begins at the start of the school year. After the school year starts, things will start moving very quickly. Don't be left behind! The world isn't perfect, and you may not have ideal circumstances as you embark upon your new vocation. Don't worry about things beyond your control and limited sphere of influence. Attend to things that you can and should do something about within your domain. Don't affix blame, fix problems. In summation, prepare as best as you can and be more concerned with making things right than assigning blame for what is wrong. Plan well and execute your tasks efficiently. Do your best, and you'll be able to sleep well at night. If you are doing your best, you'll probably be so tired in your first year that sleeping won't be a problem.

Principals are responsible for schools, and teachers' relationships with their principals are an essential component in the smooth and effective operation of schools. Principals are experienced and well-trained professional administrators who are quite knowledgeable about their school's student body and local community standards, along with the legal and ethical issues affecting both students and teachers. Most significantly, principals are responsible for student performance, as represented by standardized testing. Support the principal and be loyal to his or her administration. Principals not only look out for the students' best interests, they also look out for the teachers' best interests. Standardized testing is part of education today, and whatever techniques the principal employs to maximize student performance have probably been tried, tested, and found to be useful. Both teachers and students will benefit from good test scores.

What about your students? Although you might not know what kind of students you'll be teaching, you can be sure that they will present unique challenges, have unique personalities, and demonstrate unique skills. These students may be very diverse and represent a multitude of ethnicities, faiths, gender identities, and, along with various English language abilities, possess a wide range of physical and cognitive abilities. Treat all students with respect. Teachers do not have a mandate to judge. As an educator, you do have a mandate to teach your subject, maintain safety, establish good order, and practice sound classroom management techniques. Above all, be fair. Educate your students. Advocate for your students. Support your students. Most of all, believe in your students. People often perform as well or poorly as they are expected to perform. Expect great things from your students. Your students' success is your success.

Students often have concerned parents, or concerned persons serving in a parental function. Sadly, students might also not have any concerned adults in their lives. As a teacher, you'll have a responsibility to communicate with parents or guardians to discuss how to achieve the best educational outcomes for students. This may be difficult. Tact and patience may be required. Respect students' families. There are many value systems, and you are not getting paid to make cultural judgements. But, you are getting paid to enlist families to support their students' education. Be the concerned adult promoting education, and encourage families to support their students' education. Above all, don't be discouraged. Not every parent will be responsive. Some won't come to meetings at all. Many students may not even have parents. Remember, you can't change the whole world, but you just might make a difference in your little piece of the world. Do what you can, and don't give up.

Are you sure you're ready to actually do this? You may have noticed that the pay scale for teaching isn't, how shall we say, all that lucrative. You'll be up early every morning and often leave for school in the dark. At school, when the bell rings at three, you won't be heading for the door for a while. When you get home, you'll probably be grading homework while your spouse is watching TV. So, are you OK with some hard work? Are you ready for a challenge?

Of course you're ready! Otherwise you'd have never made it this far! Remember, teaching is a great responsibility. You know that. But, you also know there are going to be a lot of great rewards. The most important reward you'll receive is knowing that you made a difference in the world and did something tangible to make our country, state, and local community a better place. And that is something that money just can't buy!

Good luck on your new career,
John Ford

Dear Future Self,

I want to remind you of where you started. At the time of this letter, you are a full-time student working two part-time jobs, married, and raising teenagers. Your children are making life-impacting decisions, your husband and you have struggled with unemployment, you shop with food stamps, stress over paying rent, and function on minuscule amounts of sleep. You put yourself and your family through this struggle because you are an addict. Wait! Don't make a snap judgement. Read on.

You were given the chance to work at a local community college as an educational aid for special needs adult students, and it was there that you became hooked. There was an autistic student struggling with his classes, and college was a big change for him. The buildings loomed above him with its teachers and multiple students bustling all around. Every item, scent, and sound piled on copious bits of sensory information for him to process. His schedule and assignments added to his agitation. During a tutoring session, he rocked in his seat while pouring over lecture notes… and then something seemed to click for him. To see the glow of understanding in a non-neurotypical student was euphoric for you. *Your* heart raced, and *he* was elated. You wanted more!

Soon, your life revolved around pursing degrees in science education and special needs education. You knew that science courses attracted the visual thinkers, the pattern thinkers, the verbal thinkers—all kinds of variants of mental processing—and you aimed to be among them. You schemed, fixated, and romanticized as you dreamed of putting yourself in those classrooms. Eventually, you gave yourself multiple opportunities to feed on those students' elation over comprehending complex concepts and exhibiting mastery of subjects.

As you now begin your career as an educator, remember that your special needs students have unique psychological and physiological traits that influence how they experience failure and success. Some of your students will know achievement because of their abilities. Some will struggle to deal with a lifetime of punishment for simply being human. You will see other educators slight those students, and it will enrage and embroil you. However, you will also witness educators showing compassion with understanding, and I hope that inspires and empowers you.

Your students will be diverse in their thought processes. Some will be born with unique minds, and they will only know life with that type of mental processing. Others will have spent part of their lives with a non-neurotypical brain, after a traumatic injury resulted in a processing disorder. You have been given the chance to aid them in their educational careers, and I hope you are reveling in it.

I pray that you are pursuing lofty goals. Write the next study or guidelines for educating special needs students. Give training seminars for professors to augment their classroom instruction to better educate all processing types. Keep pushing for that next step, next achievement, and next accolade because, in the process, you are laying down a foundation for students that were once considered less than adequate. You now have the opportunity to show them how they can become more than great.

I have written the poem below for you, my future self. In it, I am trying to portray the feeling I described earlier when I witnessed that moment of excited understanding a special needs student had in a biology class. It was a great moment to witness, and it is a topic that I /we am/are passionate about. I want to create more of those moments, and I will do that through you.

Sincerely,
Your Current Self,
Nicole Stumbling Bear

THE BEAUTY IN THE BIOLOGY

With the edict that "life gives rise to life"
More than the brutish pursuit of procreation
Dominance and artfully won survival

It's the cleverness of color and mimicry
It's life deep down in the marrow
Felt in the rhythms of the stampede

Majestically made
Magically presented
Magnificently deadly

It is the earth welding power of the mother
The protective splendor of the father
And the star-filled heavens of the offspring

Foolish mortals search the skies for answers

Probe dust and flesh for clues

But there is a cosmos hidden in the microbe

Explore it

Explore it all!

Find the life that gives rise to your life.

Copyright © by Nicole Stumbling Bear. Reprinted by permission.

Letters Written to Novice Early Childhood and Elementary Level Educators

"We need to understand that every time an elementary teacher captures the imagination of a child through the arts or music of language, this nation gets a little stronger."

Richard W. Riley, (1933–___), former U. S. Secretary of Education (1993–2001) and governor of South Carolina (1979–1987).

Dear Younger Self,

I have not spoken to you much except when I have had those revelation moments or flashbacks from the first few years of teaching. So, this letter is from the future, the future that you thought might not be possible after that first year of teaching. Well, you made it, and just barely, but you've successfully impacted the world through the students that you've taught and poured yourself into for the last 12 years!

Yes, I know it's hard to believe, especially when you think back to the first day you walked into the school and noticed all of the beautifully decorated classrooms, and then walked a few steps further and saw your classroom with your name on the outside of the door. You were SO proud—until you walked into your classroom and saw four barren ivory colored walls and furniture all over the place! OH MY GOD! Where do I begin? As you stood there overwhelmed and trying to figure out how you were going to get your classroom to look like the classrooms you passed on the way down the hall, the teacher across the hall came and said, "Hey, we gotta hustle to the media center for the staff meeting. The principal doesn't like tardy teachers!"

Still in a daze, you stood there for a moment thinking: "What's a staff meeting! Where's the media center? Oh my gosh, do you see my classroom that has nothing in it but jumbled up furniture?" But you just followed that teacher to the media center and sat with her and a group of people who were already in what seemed to be an intense conversation that you didn't understand.

Ha-ha-ha-ha-ha-ha-ha! However, it was no laughing matter *then*, because your heart felt like it was beating a thousand times per minute, sitting at that table with other teachers that you'd never met. Sitting at that table listening to them felt like being in a new country hearing people speak in a foreign language. They were talking about AYPs, EOGs, IEPs, and other stuff that just made your eyes blink double time! WOW! You were SO overwhelmed, but as you introduced yourself, the teachers at the table started to ask if you had been to your room? You paused to think of what to say, not wanting to sound like an idiot. "Yes, I stopped by on my way to the meet- ..." —and before you could finish your sentence, they told you not to worry. They were going to help you set up your room since they had come earlier in the week to arrange their classrooms. It all worked out!

You got past *that* worry, and then began to worry about the type of teacher you were going to be, especially after hearing all about the students you were going to have in your class this year. Teachers in the building were telling you about the behavior of different students, the parents—the good, the bad, and the ugly! You found yourself driving home from school, sitting at the dinner table, and even on the weekends, thinking about every classroom scenario that could possibly happen. You used to try to stop yourself from doing that, but you realized that those thoughts helped you to anticipate questions and be proactive in planning and preparing for the school year. On top of all of that, you began to question yourself. How will I remember everything that I learned about teaching? What if I forget to include all of the learning styles? Heck, what were those again? Ha-ha-ha-ha-ha!

All of those thoughts and worries, and your students arrived, and you made it through your first year of teaching. Yes, there were some hiccups, like the time you assigned a project because you saw something similar in the classroom down the hall, but you didn't give students a rubric. As a result, your principal got that ugly note from the parent after their child got a low grade. Ouch! Well, that episode taught you that rubrics are very important because they help you to score students' work, and they help parents and students to know your expectations. Oh, and you can't ever forget the time that you called a parent in the middle of the school year to tell them how their child was misbehaving and disrupting the class, and shockingly, the parent screamed at you because they said that you only call them when their child is misbehaving. Eeek! Well, although you were upset because the parent screamed at you, you realized that no parent should only hear from a teacher when a student misbehaves, but instead, that you should call throughout the year to report good things, too!

Oh, how I wish that I would have known back when we first started what I know now. Not that I would change a whole lot because the experiences— *those hiccups*—helped you to develop into the me I now know. The challenging times, the times when you questioned your career choice, and times when you learned life-lessons through mistakes, were the times when the ground was ripe for growth and impact. I say that because, as I write this letter, I think about a vegetable garden that my students currently are growing and using to learn about many different aspects of life. When I looked at this garden earlier today, I saw the soil, the beads of water on the leaves, and the sunshine hovering over the garden. It reminded me of the process of developing as a teacher. In teaching, you've had dirt, which in the physical sense is grimy and dark in color and texture, but also has nutrients that provide nourishment for the plant. This is like the hiccups that everyone experiences in any career, but these times, much like the soil, have a way of nourishing and strengthening our faith to believe that our work is important to the survival of our garden of students. I thought about the beads of rain, and how rain naturally flows down and refreshes the garden to help the vegetation thrive at different points during the growth process. This can be likened to the times when your students' level of mastery continues to grow, or when your teammate tells you how great a job you're doing, or when a parent comes to a conference and cries because their child has hated school until this year, after having *you* for a teacher! Then, I thought about the sunshine and how it was hovering over the garden. This, to me, represented the beauty of teaching.

As I looked at the garden, the colors were bright and the beautiful blossoms were hanging over the borders of the garden. This beautiful garden is the result of soil nourishing, water refreshing, and sunlight giving energy to the plants. In other words, everything and every experience working together for the purpose of developing the best plant from the potential of a seed. Those beautiful plants are not just a part of a garden, but a life cycle that extends beyond the boundaries of the garden. Much like your impact as a teacher has extended beyond the four walls of a classroom and into the world!

You were designed for a purpose and all of your experiences have worked together to create the YOU that now coaches and inspires beginning teachers to continue to impact the world every day for a greater tomorrow! Some would say,

"If I could turn back the hands of time, I would do things differently." I say there's no need to turn back the hands of time, just enjoy each moment, each student, each lesson, and each experience, because it all works together and is a piece in your ever-evolving puzzle called life!

Sincerely,
Ever-Evolving You,
LaTonya Gaines-Montgomery

Dear Mikey,

I can so clearly see you walking around our first classroom on that hot August morning before your very first day of teaching. Pacing back and forth while reading over your plans, stopping to pick up a piece of paper on the floor, moving the picture frames on the desk, and straightening your tie (you will quit wearing those in about three years). I can still remember how exciting it was to hear those footsteps coming down the hall and to see those Kindergarteners all burst into the room. Enjoy the naps, making snacks with the kids, and having an assistant—those days are numbered. These are the days that you will remember as the "good old days" when you get older.

At this moment in time, you are all potential. The possibilities are endless. I'm sitting here 20 years later, still thinking that the possibilities are boundless. You will make hundreds of decisions each day that will impact your future both in and out of the classroom. Make the most of every day. Know that, throughout your career, you will maintain that you were always in the right place—at the right time.

Keep your easygoing style—this will serve you well. You have a unique ability to modify and adjust to the "opportunities" that are thrown your way. You will be able to handle anything that comes your way along this path you have chosen.

That little quirky touch of obsessive-compulsive disorder (OCD) that you have will definitely serve you well at school and on various boards and committees in the coming years. Procedures and routines will help you create five year olds that can file their own work, check out books from the classroom library, keep supplies neatly arranged in color-coded bins, and accurately clean up and put away center materials. While these are all great manifestations of your orderly nature—you may want to work on that hang up you have about folding your clothes as they go in the basket to be washed . . . nobody has time for that anyway. You will eventually let that habit go—along with making sure the trash cans are empty every time you leave the house . . . Leaving for a trip or vacation is a different story . . .

Procedures and routines will be so valuable to you in your educational life. You will utilize some of the same routines throughout your career—how to collect papers, how or when to sharpen a pencil, how to shake someone's hand, how to greet a guest or visitor, center rotations or clean up, and general classroom expectations or maintenance of space. The students will rise to your expectations every time in this arena—even the fifth graders that you will love teaching one day. I know that is hard to believe as you await the arrival of your kindergarteners, but you will one day relish the time spent with your upper elementary students. The "no gray area" of your personality will help you enforce the procedures and routines along with your behavior expectations, and together will create a classroom environment that suits you perfectly, while being warm and open.

Take a deep breath—you will find some things overwhelming at times, but you will be able to handle everything that comes your way. Your faith, friends, family, and hobbies will be there with you to carry you through the darker times and celebrate all the good times. Your passion for gardening will turn out to be an asset in the classroom. You will use this hobby to reach many students and to spark an interest in a few that may not have otherwise been reached. Horticulturalist will become a coveted weekly job in your classroom—by the way, I still have the plant that is sitting on the corner of your bookcase right now. That plant has seen us through three school systems, four schools, twenty years, and hundreds of students.

You always seem to end up at the right place at the right time. Continue to follow your heart when faced with these decisions. You will teach in a variety of schools and in a couple of different capacities. Each of these phases will remind you of why you started teaching and what you enjoy the most. Stay true to you, and be yourself. Your love of learning, reading, gardening, and cooking will serve you well in the future, in and out of school.

You will learn many things from your colleagues over the years—wonderful and horrible ideas, suggestions, habits, and attitudes. Always filter these items by asking, "Is this what is best for my students?" Know that you will also see some ideas cycle back through the field of education. Hang on to what is best for children. Continue to read and research. You are destined to be that "life-long learner" that we have been hearing so much about recently.

Stay true to yourself. The manners and ideals that you grew up with will serve you well and open many doors in the future. However, you will quickly learn that not everyone had the same experiences in childhood. You will teach students that have faced more in their short lives than you have in two or three times as long.

Stay out of the lounge. Once you identify the grumpy, grumbly group, stay away from them. They do not want to hear about your great newly discovered teaching strategy, the new organizational items you bought, the new grant you just received—or anything else. Just leave them alone. They are looking for someone to commiserate with, not someone to suggest solutions for their problems. Be the optimist. You will always like having the proverbial glass at least half full.

You will meet many interesting people both in and out of school. Learn from them. Ask questions or try new things—except shellfish—you are still allergic to all shellfish. Continue to push your students to learn and dream beyond their current situation. Encourage them to reach past their immediate circumstances and limitations. Push them to keep moving forward, even when you are ready to give up on them.

Keep the funny notes. There will be days that you need to laugh to keep from crying or screaming (you are really more likely to just stop at a store after school and get ice cream or wine, but that's a different story, too). Treasure the "best" teacher notes and the thank-you notes. You will always smile as you read these and look at the drawings. Keep the parent notes. You will treasure a few of these—and deeply reflect on several as well.

Be a risk taker. You will learn to ask for forgiveness instead of permission in your career. You will take several leaps of faith that will all work out to your benefit and the greater good. Be ready and jump when these opportunities come along.

Above all, trust yourself . . . well, except for clothing and hairstyle choices. We will not look good with highlighted and feathered hair or the mustache, and we don't have time to visit the vest and plaid shirt issues. You know that you are better than anyone else. Stay true to yourself. Do what you deep down know beyond a doubt is good for your students. Don't fall for the pastel suits with matching shoes either . . . Those pictures still haunt us. You will make some amazing friends along the way that will help with the clothing choice issues, if you will listen to them. Don't just smile and nod, but LISTEN, or forever be reminded that you owned a peach suit with blue pinstripes.

Try every crazy thing that you can think of to do . . . You will create a village, a marketplace, a train, an igloo, a waterfall, a jungle, and many other wonderful things in your room over the years. Embrace your creative spirit, and when you see that same spirit in your colleagues, encourage them to express their own ideas in fun and unique ways. You will make several amazing friends this way.

You will fail, you will embarrass yourself, you will be wrong. Respond with grace and humility. Make an apology if it is warranted. You will be surprised at the result of this action.

My final thought for *you*, *me*, and *us* is to keep working to be that teacher that we wanted to be on the first day of school. Push your students, support them in their academic efforts, and provide them the scaffolding to build their future. It seems simple and idealistic to say, but many of our future students just need to know that we care about them and are willing to fight for them.

I will not keep you any longer. I know you need to rearrange the pillows in the reading center—AGAIN—and adjust the blinds on the window, and check to make sure that your tie is still straight and neatly aligned with your tie clip and belt buckle, so-o-o-o . . . Good luck!! You will be amazing today . . .

Have a great day of learning,
Michael C. Luther

Dear Younger Me,

Congratulations, you are about to begin an amazing and incredibly rewarding educational journey! The future is difficult to predict, but I can say with certainty that, in the field of education, you will spend many more years learning, growing, and—equally as important in my mind—having fun! Education is often defined as the imparting and acquiring of knowledge through teaching and learning; you will never stop learning in the education profession! The memories you will help create and experience are both priceless and unimaginable.

You will never forget your first teaching job. The week before school started, I (you) worked tirelessly to prepare for my students' arrival. I remember asking the experienced colleagues, members of my team, "What words of wisdom do you have for me?" One teacher said, "You can get students to do what you want, but if you show them you care, by being patient (sometimes that is *really* hard) and treating them with respect, they will work harder than you could possibly imagine. After all, you can pay a person to teach, but you can't pay them to care." I soon realized that meant to **love first and teach second**.

My students in that first year were well below the state average academically as they struggled to read, write, and perform basic mathematics skills. They were also well below the poverty line—not some, but all. But guess what? I did not care because I finally had my own students, and I was determined to make a difference!

I remember calling my own parents to share stories about my students. One story was about Natalie and how bossy she was to the other students. My mom quickly reminded me of how bossy I was as a young girl.

Slowly but surely, my students began to make gains. It was so exhausting; I worked every night and every weekend. Any money I did not spend on bills, I would use to buy pencils, paper, scissors, and snacks for my students. We were all learning together and having so much fun. I looked forward to going to school and seeing my students every day.

Over time, the long hours took a toll on my health, and I became sick. When I returned to school, I found notes from my students. I was somewhat shocked to see a note from Otis, because he did not like to write, primarily because it was such a struggle for him. Otis was an undernourished African-American boy with big brown eyes and a smile that could melt your heart. He was quiet, but when he did speak, it was with a slow, soft southern drawl.

As I read Otis' letter, tears filled my eyes. His message did not demonstrate the mastery of capitalization and punctuation. His meaning however was nevertheless clear and deeply appreciated. He did not just miss me, but he missed and loved me "so bad!" I remember thinking, my students must recognize how much I care about them. They each held a special place in my heart. It is hard to imagine you could love your students so much. I did not have children of my own, so I had never experienced the power of this extraordinary kind of love before. I was overwhelmed by my students' heartfelt letters. I embraced **love first and teach second**.

Mynery niceteacheris happy she,BesickI miss herso badand she. Isanice teacherand Iloveher Sobad By Otis

After my first year, I could not help but wonder, "Did I do enough? Did I make a difference? Could I have done more?" There was a steep learning curve. I was filled with a sense of inadequacy as a teacher. I still had so much to learn. I wanted to be better, which motivated me to go back to school that very next summer. I needed to continue my education. I had to learn more to make a difference. I was eager to absorb the issues of curriculum, instruction, and assessments. I thought about school culture and classroom management with a whole new perspective.

The following year, I found myself teaching in a very diverse school. I had students from various socio-economic backgrounds. What a challenge—but I was ready! I had a new teaching mindset, and I was so much more prepared for this school year. After all, I was older and wiser, or so I thought.

We had been in school for about a month when Carl fell asleep in class. How dare him! I spent so much time on my lesson plans, and they were good. I even stayed late the day before to clean the room and change our classroom bulletin boards. At first, I ignored his behavior, thinking maybe he just wanted attention. The next day, same thing, asleep again! I had a great engaging task, and how about my new bulletin boards? This time I walked over and gently tapped him on his shoulder, telling him to sit up. I would not have students sleeping in my class. Those high expectations are essential. I was taught that in my teacher education course! Next day, asleep again, and his whole demeanor had changed over the week. He came to class exhausted and irritable. He also had become very unpleasant toward the other students. I was totally frustrated with his behavior, so by the end of the week, I finally decided to pull him aside and talk with him. I took time from my busy, demanding schedule and spoke with this student, one-on-one. As we began to talk about his behavior, I demanded an explanation. Tears began streaming down his cheeks as he shared his story. His mother, helplessly in the grasp of drug abuse, attempted suicide in the presence of him and two-year-old twin brothers. He had been staying up late to care for his brothers. I was in total shock, even overwhelmed. It had taken me a week to talk with this student, to understand his plight. He needed someone to care. I could not believe I had forgotten my first words of advice, **love first and teach second.** I had gotten so caught up in my everyday frustrations due to the lack of resources, the endless amount of paperwork, and demands to master standards that I forgot what is truly important: the students. I thought, "I am inadequate. How could I let this happen? I have so much to learn!"

I have spent most of my summers in school over the years. I attend workshops or conferences to become a better educator. I want to be the best for my students. I think it is because I care so much for my students. It has motivated me to continue to develop as a teacher. I have sought opportunities to learn and have had many fortunate experiences to be trained by some of our nation's leaders. The more I learn, the more I realize there is still so much to learn. As my teaching evolved, I truly began to **love first and teach second.** Year after year, I became amazed at how students progressed. I created a risk-free culture for learning. Students were provided high-leverage tasks, and they rose to the challenge.

I have learned over the years in the field of education that you are never really totally prepared. I would think I had it all under control, but then something would happen, and that all too familiar feeling of being overwhelmed would hit me like a ton of bricks. I now believe if you don't feel somewhat inadequate, you are probably not doing a good job. Think about all the stresses placed on teachers. The feeling of being overwhelmed is probably not a lack of preparedness; it is an entirely reasonable response to the demands put on teachers. We must acknowledge that feeling of being overwhelmed or inadequate. We must use these feelings to motivate our learning so we can continue to grow to be the best teacher for our students. So, I think it is perfectly acceptable to feel overwhelmed or inadequate at times.

As you begin the next step in your teaching profession, think about Natalie, Otis, and Carl, and remember to **love first and teach second**, and please keep learning! As I complete my 30th year in education, I am currently in the process of finishing a doctoral degree, still learning and growing, still feeling overwhelmed and inadequate at times.

Never Forget: **Love First and Teach Second**,

Older Experienced Me
Kitty C. Rutherford

Dearest Laura,

I wish you knew what I know now about teaching when you first stepped into that first grade classroom south of Oakland, CA. Remember? It was your first teaching job and your classroom was filled with 33 students who represented 7 different languages and cultures, and 8 of the students were identified as having English as a Second Language (ESL) that were pulled two times a day for services. Remember? Remember all the joys of reading out loud and daily writing journals, field trips all around Bay Area, and watching a student independently read for the first time? Do you remember all the challenges? Oh, how can you forget? Remember how tired you were at the end of each day and how tough it was to get along with some of your colleagues? Remember how your heart broke when the ESL teacher would knock on the classroom door to pick up your students, who, by law, had to leave the whole-class, literacy-rich content area activity that you knew they would never get a chance to experience again? Oh, Dearest Laura, if you only knew then—what I know now—about teaching.

Well, in an attempt to communicate my best advice to you—what I know now about teaching, I have chosen to write a letter to you in a list format of the 10 most important pieces of advice that I have to give to you. Although this format may seem cold and impersonal, I really believe that it is the best format to communicate to you in! After all, not only have lists saved my sanity as a teacher (and as a mother of six), but they have also helped me to become the confident educator that I am today! So, here it goes:

1. **Stay Organized:** Dearest Laura, Stay Organized! Make lists for everything that you do and communicate the information on them to the people who need to know! This may seem simple, but in the fast and ever-changing world of technology and with teachers being tasked with more and more things to do, staying organized is critical to effective teaching. Remember what Karen, your grade-level mentor in CA taught you? To keep multiple copies of the class list updated and printed off and ready to use at a moment's notice, to complete head counts on a field trip, or to keep track of how many times you asked each student a direct question each week in the classroom? Stay organized in all that you do because it will help you

to succeed, both in and out of the classroom. Today, I am a mother of six children (can you believe it?), and I stay organized by keeping a monthly family calendar hanging on the wall for all to see, as well as a small pocket calendar containing duplicate information in my purse that I carry around with me throughout the day. Today, I am also a professor (what do you think of that?) of education at a university and not only do I have a monthly calendar for them, too, but I also begin each week with Monday Morning Announcements that are sent to each class on my schedule that semester. This way, our classroom community is always on the same page with respect to assignment requirements and due dates, service learning opportunities, and other important details and reminders. And yes . . . it is in list format (just like this one!).

2. **Smile:** Dearest Laura, Smile! Oh, I wish that I had done this more throughout my life as a teacher and as a mother. One of the most famous mothers of all, Mother Teresa, once said, "Every time you smile at someone, it is an action of love, a gift to that person, a beautiful thing." Dearest Laura, greet your own children, your colleagues, the students that you teach, and all the parents and guardians that love them, with the gift of a smile. So simple, really, but what a different world this would be if we all smiled just a little bit more.

3. **Read, Read, Read!** Dearest Laura, Read, Read, Read! I cannot emphasize this piece of advice enough—for parents and for teachers! You learned about the power of reading out loud in your undergraduate education, so hold this knowledge dear to your heart and, over the years, intentionally engage in

reading out loud at home with your children, at school with your students, at the university level with your pre-service teachers, and with your colleagues at professional conferences and presentations. Reading books out loud remains at the heart of teaching, and the benefits, as you know, are numerous. Below I share just a few:

- Reading out loud is enjoyable.
- Reading out loud increases motivation.
- Reading out loud accesses complicated text.
- Reading out loud exposes rich vocabulary.
- Reading out loud provides a fluent reading role model.
- Reading out loud reinforces oral fluency.
- Reading out loud teaches anything from phonemic awareness to the Underground Railroad, and from adjectives to the water cycle.
- Reading out loud introduces people, animals, nature, and cultures from around the world.
- Reading out loud aids in comprehension, connections, and discussions.
- Reading out loud contributes positively to classroom management.

Dearest Laura, READ ON!!!!! Give the gift of reading out loud to your children at home and to your students in your reading specialist, K-5, and university classrooms, and to your colleagues at professional conferences! It will serve you and others well! I promise!

4. **Favorite Read-Aloud Books:** Dearest Laura, Develop a library and a list of favorite read-aloud books! Remember how a colleague from New Zealand encouraged you to have a favorite children's book to read out loud way back in 1993 and that it would be a great idea to keep a list of favorite read-aloud books? Do you remember the first book on your list (Tacky the Penguin by Helen Lester) and how many times you read it over and over and over to students of all ages? Well, that was great advice, and I encourage you to keep

adding to your list of favorite read-aloud books as you come across them. Below are five of my favorite read-aloud books from over the years that are appropriate for any age and are in no particular order. Go out and buy them and read them to every student and parent and colleague that you can! Read! Read! Read!

Henry's Freedom Box by Ellen Levine and Kadir Nelson is a book about a famous slave who mailed himself to freedom.

Tacky the Penguin by Helen Lester is a book about a penguin named Tacky who is an odd bird but a very nice bird to have around. Everybody is different.

Leo the Late Bloomer by Robert Krauss is a book about a lion cub who learns to read, write, and speak in his own developmental time.

Faithful Elephants: A True Story of People, Animals, and War by Yukio Tsuchiya is a book about the horrors of WW II at the Ueno Zoo in Tokyo, Japan.

Yo! Yes? by Chris Raschka is a book about two friends told in very few words.

5. **Dr. Allington's SIX Non-Negotiables:** Dearest Laura, Do you remember reading the first edition of Dr. Allington's book, Classrooms That Work, in the early 1990s? Well, it is now on its sixth edition, and I encourage you to continue reading the work of Dr. Allington because his research will continue to inspire you and guide your teaching every step of the way. (Fun Fact: You will have the opportunity to see him and talk to him at conferences around the country, correspond with him via email, and even have lunch with him in Knoxville, TN in 2016!!!) Of all the research of his that will inspire you, be sure to embrace the following six non-negotiables for teaching reading that students need to do every day:

1. Listen to an adult read out loud.
2. Read something they understand.
3. Read something accurately.
4. Read something that they like.
5. Write something meaningful.
6. Talk about what they read and/or write.

This research is powerful and practical and provides teachers a way to crosscheck what is happening in their classrooms with respect to reading and writing. At some point in your teaching journey, if you observe that your students are not reading and writing as well as you would like, ask yourself: Am I reading to them every day? Are they reading something that they can understand, read accurately, and that they like? Are they writing and talking every day? If not, then something in your classroom needs changing!

6. **Three Questions for Reflection:** Dearest Laura, Reflect on everything that you do! As a professor of education, there are three questions that guide my students as they reflect on every teaching decision they make:

   • What did I do?
   • Why did I do it?
   • Did it work? If not—make changes!

Dearest Laura, I wish I had been taught how to efficiently reflect on my teaching decisions when I was a young teacher just starting out. That would have been so helpful when I encountered difficult situations throughout the years.

7. **Share:** Dearest Laura, Share your best ideas with others and they will share their best ideas with you! Trust me on this one.

8. **Take Risks:** Dearest Laura, Take Risks! Don't be afraid to try new things (I highly suggest that you read the book, <u>Scaredy Squirrel</u>, by Melanie Watt. You will love it and so will your students!). Don't stagnate and teach the same way by doing the same thing over and over and over again. Read the research, pay attention during your staff development trainings, and figure out a way to try something new. And when you do, reflect using the three questions above. Don't be like Scaredy Squirrel; get out of your nut tree!! You just might surprise yourself!

9. **Change What You Can:** Dearest Laura, Change what you can and don't get too upset about what you can't. For example, one year when I taught third grade in San Antonio, TX, our district spent thousands and thousands of dollars on test preparation booklets for the TAAS test my students were going to have to take in the spring. I was not a big fan of these booklets, but I couldn't change the fact that they were expensive, delivered, and sitting in my classroom. I was also under direct orders from my principal to use them— period. Some of my third grade colleagues used them in place of their entire reading curriculum for months. Instead, I kept my reading curriculum and used the booklets for only 15 minutes each day after our morning routine. Change what you can and don't get too upset about what you can't.

10. **Love:** Dearest Laura, Above all—LOVE your students. It makes all the difference in the world.

Dearest Laura, what I just shared with you is the best advice that I have as I reflect back on my younger self. I can assure you that you have chosen the best career in the world and, even after 25 years, I can say with confidence that I cannot imagine my life without the joys and challenges of being a teacher.

Please consider heeding my heartfelt advice of *staying organized, smiling, reading, keeping lists of great read-alouds, following Dr. Allington's brilliant research, reflecting, sharing, taking risks, changing what you can,* and above all—*loving those around you, especially your students.*

With Love (more than a quarter of a century later),

Dr. Laura A. Staal

References

Cunningham, P. M., & Allington, R. L. (2003). *Classrooms that work: They can all read and write*. Boston: Allyn and Bacon.

Kraus, R., & Aruego, J. (1971). *Leo the late bloomer.*

Lester, H., Munsinger, L., Zara, L., & National Braille Press. (2006). *Tacky the penguin*. Boston, MA: National Braille Press.

Levine, E., & Nelson, K. (2007). *Henry's freedom box*. New York: Scholastic Press.

Raschka, C., Sporn, M., & Weston Woods Studios. (2000). *Yo! Yes?*. Westport, CT: Weston Woods.

Tsuchiya, Y., & Lewin, T. (1988). *Faithful elephants: A true story of animals, people, and war.*

Watt, M. (2006). *Scaredy squirrel*. Toronto: Kids Can Press.

Instead of penning a letter, this writer chose to compose a poem to convey to the first-year teacher she once was, the insights she has gained during a long career in education.

Remembrances of Your First Year of Teaching
Written by Misty Hathcock

It's hard to put into words, but I will try

To capture remembrances of your first teaching year gone by

It wasn't easy but you persevered and kept moving on

Stayed resilient in your faith, true to your values, and finished strong

I remember your youth and vitality—you still had much to learn

Your eagerness to do your best—excellence you would yearn

I remember your love for children and advocacy for what was best

Your passion, competence, and enduring zest

I remember your knowledge of content and planning prepared you well

Your professionalism, proactiveness, and accepting of feedback helped you to excel

I remember your classroom management put you to the test

Your consistency and persistence went beyond the rest

I remember your use of technology and creativity abound

Your awareness of how your students learned and their attention you found

I remember your willingness to take risks and fail

Your motivation to ask questions, listen to different points of view, and not bail

I remember your compassion, thoughtfulness, and care

Your sincerity, tenacity, and generosity to share

I remember your vigor, enthusiasm, and fashionista style

Your honesty, authenticity, and infectious smile

I remember your straightforwardness and organization to the hilt

Your true colors, candor, and nothing left to kilt

I remember your style of doing things and living life your own way

Your sense of devotion and even a bit of play

I remember your positive nature and liveliness no one could surpass

Your dedication and commitment is truly one of class

I remember your attention to detail, faithfulness, and zeal

Your encouragement and inspiration—you ARE the real deal

I remember your loyalty to family was always number one

Your enduring fervor left nothing undone

I hope you will remember the good of present and past

The times you've touched a child's life will be precious memories that last

It's time to celebrate and prepare for the next teaching year

Remembering all the lessons learned and successes you hold dear

Thank you for teaching—the greatest profession of all

YOU were born a teacher—it was the right call!

Fall 2005

Dear First-Year Teacher Lisa,

You did not make a mistake. You were meant to do this job. You *CAN* do this job. Some days will be tougher than others. The demands of teaching are going to seem unrealistic at times. Right now, it seems like the odds are stacked against you and that you will never feel like you are doing enough, but just hang in there. Being a first year teacher in a new state is challenging, but you have never shied away from a challenge before. You were made for this role. Persevere and power through!

Stop doubting yourself and your abilities. It takes time to hone your craft. No one expects you to be an expert. You are your own toughest critic. Breathe and relax. Keep finding ways to connect with your students. You are getting better and better each day. In this first year, you will learn a tremendous amount about things that college courses and student teaching could never teach you, because you just need to experience it. You will realize the importance of having strong classroom management skills, organization in all aspects of life, and that building relationships is truly at the heart of a teacher's job. Learn all you can about your students, realize that you are working in partnership with families, and connect with educators. You will learn so much from them, and they will learn from you, too.

You are working hard. I know you are tired because you are giving it your all each and every day. It can be frustrating because you aren't seeing results as quickly as you would like. Be patient. You *will* continue to grow and improve every year. Your students will grow in ways beyond the academics. In fact, in just a few short months, you will be named the First-Year Teacher of the Year for your school. In three years, you will be recognized as the Teacher of the Year for your school. Yes, I am serious! You have what it takes to be great, and your students need you, so dry your eyes and know that one bad day does not define you as a teacher; tomorrow will be a fresh slate and a chance to learn, connect, and grow alongside your students.

The effect you have on your current class of third graders will last well beyond this school year! They will send you emails when they are in high school to let you know how much they loved being in your class, even if they do not always show it. They will go on and become successful and want to share their lives with a teacher who left a lasting impression. This class will not be the only one. You have dozens of other students who will fondly remember you as a great teacher who believed in them and made learning fun.

Expanding your Professional Learning Network, or PLN, will have the greatest impact on your teaching abilities and on your students. The relationships you form with educators at your school, in your district, and across the country will make you exponentially stronger and open your mind to many different strategies and resources for engaging your students. Instruction will shift from more teacher-centered to more student-centered, your toolbox of strategies will overflow, and you will be well equipped to meet the academic, social, and emotional needs of any student who is lucky enough to cross your path. You will soon emerge as a teacher leader and your ability to meaningfully connect with students, teachers, parents, and administrators will be one of your greatest strengths and keys to success.

So, Lisa, teach your heart out, love your students, connect with other teachers, and do your thing. You've got this! The best is yet to come. You matter, and you make a difference and will continue to do so for many more years!

Rooting you on,
Experienced and Accomplished Lisa
(Lisa Pagano)

Dear Mrs. "I Got This and Sometimes I Don't Got This,"

You are *SO* excited and nervous. Finally, you get to do—and actually get paid for—what you've always wanted to do... *TEACH*!

Remember those days when you were pretending to be a teacher and taught your dolls and stuffed animals and eventually moved up to teaching younger cousins? Well, that was great practice, but really . . . Who can't handle 4 cousins, versus 24 students? Reality is a whole new ballgame. Every year, you get to decorate and then take down all your "pretty" educational stuff off your classroom walls so someone can paint. Then, when you return year after year, you rehang some "oldies" and then add some "newbies" to your <u>not</u> newly painted walls. And if you're lucky, you will get to move all your stuff to new classrooms, say 7 or 8 times, by the time you teach 20 years.

Every year is a new experience. Something different. New students and maybe even some of the same ones if you move up to teach them in a higher grade. You actually could have written a book entitled, "Kids Say and Do the Darndest Things," but you didn't, because you were too busy teaching. That's right. You are all about your job. You think constantly about what's going on with your students and how to help them become better students. You get upset when you feel like someone didn't do right by them, or if you, as the teacher, work hard, and they, as students, don't. And sometimes you even hear their voices when you sleep. And your family just doesn't understand your commitment to your job. Your husband says, "Don't bring that home." Your oldest son says, "Don't fuss at me because those kids got on your nerves today." And the baby boy says, "Why can't you buy me a cell phone? You just bought your students at school some stuff." Yeah, a few packs of cute pencils and red pens to help me grade all that homework I just <u>have</u> to give. Otherwise, how are they learning at home? And

I only buy "stuff" they really need, like shaving cream for "Snowy Day" walks and noodles and plates to display the lifecycle of a butterfly. It's called: "Making memories of fun learning." That's priceless! Ask any good, effective teacher. They don't do their job for the money. They do it because they are excited about the changes they see in their students from August until June. That, and those summers off and great vacation days with pay! Right!

Could you even imagine yourself in a job that was boring? The same thing day in and day out? No! And that's why you teach. On days when you want to give up, think about all the lives you've affected. That point when their lightbulb came on and they learned something new. Remember the smiles and hugs. The, "I miss your class. You were a great teacher." It will happen, if you put your heart and soul into what you do and make it important to your students. But I promise you, there will be that one class that makes you want to quit and change your job title. And no matter how hard you try, you can't change the predicament you are in. Sometimes there are little people that just weren't supposed to be put together for hours at a time in the same place. But it happens, and they just can't get along, and your whole class becomes simply put . . . tolerable. You drag yourself out of bed daily and wonder: "What, oh what, will they do or say today?" And you learn to do the best you can, pray about it, and count down the days until June. And guess what? You survive!

Over time, you will get fed up with the decisions from the bosses upstairs, but it is what it is. You will have to go with the flow, adapt until the other new thing comes along, and decide which battles are worth fighting for. And the longer you teach, the harder it will become, because societies' priorities will change. A child's education will not seem that important. Facebook will occupy countless hours, when learning from a parent should've taken place. But you can't let that stop you. You have to be your students' voice. You have to show them that having a good education will take them far in life. Talk to them about what's going on in the "real world." What are they going to do when they grow up? How are they going to take care of their family? How will they make the money they need to, to go on a nice vacation? Sometimes it may not seem like they're listening, but believe me they are, and most of them will thank you for it later in life. And it's a fact . . . "Sometimes you got this, and sometimes you don't." That's the life of a teacher. But that's not what matters. What matters is how you made a difference in the lives of your students. You rock girl, and don't you ever forget it!

Yours Forever until Retirement,
Rhonda It'll Be Alright
(Rhonda Strickland Dial)

Dear Me,

Oh my! The greeting I chose for this letter is in itself a loaded statement! Is it a salutation, or is it an exclamation of distress? Perhaps by the end of this letter we will both know!

It's been twenty plus years since the first day I walked into my very own classroom, but I remember it as if it was just yesterday. I remember the joy, excitement, apprehension, fear, and concern I had the first day I walked into the classroom. To add to all of that, I was assuming the reins of a classroom that had been established by another teacher. I always felt that I had to compete against the image of the teacher before me. So, one of the first things that I have learned is to not compare, unless you're doing math or writing similes or metaphors!

When you compare yourself to others, you stop being yourself. You cannot be an effective teacher if you are more concentrated on being someone else than you are concentrated on your students and the lessons you are teaching. This is not to say that you cannot or should not pull great qualities and strategies from other teachers. You learn by observing others and using traits you have learned from others. I'm saying that you should not try to *be* that teacher. You need to *be you* and let others be themselves.

The first year of teaching can be very stressful if you let it. Don't let it. Instead, find yourself a mentor, or better yet, find yourself a friend. Sometimes a mentor is only concerned about the rules, regulations, and the goals they must meet as required for those serving as a mentor. That does not make a person an ineffective or a "bad" mentor. It just can cause that mentor to miss what is happening to you, the person. Learning the ropes as a teacher is a must. However, if you lose sight of yourself, you will become ineffective and be unable to connect to your students and your coworkers and teammates. Connections, better known as relationships, are an important part of life. You need support and encouragement to make it through life. Only by being yourself can you develop honest and lasting relationships. A friend fits the bill for this. A mentor that becomes a friend is the best of both worlds.

As you develop these relationships, keep everything in perspective. One of the best pieces of advice I was given was from my wonderful husband, Stan. The day before I started work, he told me that I could, "love them, care about them, and care for them, but under no circumstances can you bring them home!" You will come across students whose lives will tear at your heart. You cannot become too caught up in their lives. You can counsel them, conference with their parents, seek outside assistance, and be there to listen, but never become so consumed by or involved in their lives that you become biased and incapable of separating the situation from the child. As challenging as that will be—and it *WILL* be challenging—nurture and be compassionate, but your primary goal is to teach the children in your charge. Teach them more than academics, though. Teach them to be compassionate, forgiving, helpful, thoughtful, courageous, and independent. These are all characteristics of being productive and contributing citizens in their community and nation.

Do not think for one moment that you should not do all that you can to assist a child who faces struggles in his or her personal life. After all, even though our degree is in education, we are also parent, nurse, doctor, counselor, psychologist, and confidante. We just need to be sure that we keep a good balance between personal and professional life. Maintenance of this separation will save a lot of trouble in the long run. There are professionals that are licensed and/or certified to handle those types of situations. Utilize them. Listen to them. So, cultivate a relationship with these professionals.

The first people with whom you want to develop a relationship are the secretarial/office and custodial staff. These are the people who really run the school. The secretarial/office staff handle your time/payroll, oversee the money for supplies, and have the heartbeat of the school. They can help you with any problem you have at school. They know everyone. They also have the ear of the administrators. A positive recommendation from these staff members can do a lot to open doors for you. Just be kind to them. Always speak and smile. Turn in paperwork correctly and on time. By no means am I suggesting that you suck up to or brown-nose them. They can see that from a mile away. Just be courteous and respectful. They work with you and not for you. The same applies for custodians.

They do those menial tasks none of us want to do, like cleaning bathrooms; sweeping, mopping, and waxing floors; cutting the grass; and cleaning up vomit. They keep the school clean and orderly. They are there before you get there and leave after you do. They work with you. They are not your servants. Do not think of ordering them around or demanding things from them. Instead, treat them with the utmost respect. Ask them for help and never demand it. Show gratitude to them for all they do for you, and they will be more willing to do more for you.

Being kind and courteous works for everyone. However, it is not always easy to maintain that attitude. Sometimes you come across students who do not understand what that means. They have lived in an environment that teaches them that selfishness and violence are the only way to get ahead in life. You will be tempted to show them that type of treatment because that is all that they understand. You must always remember that you are the adult in the situation, and as such, you must set and maintain the standard in your classroom. Will you lose your temper sometimes? Yes, you will! Even when that happens, you must use it as a lesson to teach your students the better way to handle those situations. I do not have a soft sweet voice. My voice is loud and the more excited I get, the louder I become. Try as I might, I have not been able to develop that soft, low voice. Therefore, I "warn" my students at the beginning of the year. I even show them the difference between my loud normal voice and my boisterous angry voice. I yell to show them what it sounds like when I do yell. They need to know and understand the difference so that they will not think that I am yelling at them all day long. Some students will come to you from a household that barely speaks above a whisper, so a voice of any volume beyond a whisper will be a cultural shock to them. You must help them to understand that a voice that is loud does not necessarily mean anger or unkindness.

Usually that works out. Should it not work, do not take it personally. Do the best you can, and pray that the year will pass without a lot of upset.

At the same time, there will be students who come from an environment of loud, boisterous talk and some violence. Showing kindness and gentleness is the best way to show them the other side of life. They must learn that yelling and screaming are not the way to show love and kindness. Pushing, shoving, and hitting are not the way to show love either. You will see this, especially with the boys. They are just being boys, but they must be shown and taught better ways. So quickly these actions can go from play to fighting, because not all boys understand that this is just a macho way of developing into manhood. Help them to learn these things without damaging or humiliating them. One important note here—should you ever correct a student and then find out that you were wrong, please apologize. If you correct in front of the entire class, apologize in front of the entire class. You will show you are human and make mistakes while gaining a new level of respect from your students.

So I have addressed not comparing yourself to other teachers, being kind, appreciative, and respectful to the office staff or secretaries and custodians, and what to expect from your students and how to deal with them. Now for the biggie—PAPERWORK! This includes grading papers, lesson plans, and all the official paperwork you are required to do. It is so easy to be consumed by all of this. It will appear that your paperwork reproduces and procreates overnight, but it really doesn't! It doesn't, however, take much for it to get out of hand! The one thing you want to do, and stick with it, is to set aside non-negotiable time for paperwork. Any forms that you need to submit to the office, forms for student evaluation or achievement or behavior assessment, demographic forms, etc., should all have a set time of day each day, or they will become in charge of you. When you get behind in that type of paperwork, it wreaks havoc with your day-to-day plans and paper grading. Contrary to popular belief, YOU NEVER CATCH UP! NEVER! Your best bet is to never get behind. This comes from someone who has adult ADHD (Attention Deficit Hyperactivity Disorder). It seems the older I get, the more prevalent it has become. Not being the most organized person in the world does not help. If there is one thing that I would insist on for my beginning teacher me is to develop organizational skills that become second nature to me. It would keep the paperwork tamed and the papers in my classroom under control.

Lesson plans are another thorn in my side. I am not sure why veteran teachers are held to the same standard as beginning teachers in this area, but we are. I think that veteran teachers should be trusted to know what they are teaching and how they will teach it; therefore, they should be allowed a different type of lesson plan than the beginning or novice teacher. However, if a veteran teacher is deemed ineffective or lessons do not seem to be organized, then that teacher should be put on an action plan and be required to do what beginning teachers do. I'm just saying . . . Anyway, back to the subject at hand. Lesson plans are a very necessary and useful tool of teaching. Do not be afraid to plan with others to get this done. Collaboration makes lesson plans easier to do and more creative, challenging, and appealing to the students. A different perspective is often what is needed to add spice to a lesson. Besides, you will not be strong in every subject area. If you are, you need to be writing books on lesson plans or become the lead teacher, or better yet, transfer to central office. You are needed there! Whatever your weakness, find someone that has your weakness as their strength, and then work together with that person to do phenomenal things! Do not be afraid to share. Just make sure you are sharing and not doing the lessons for everyone else. There will always be someone who will ride your coattails and not be a contributor. Have a heart-to-heart conversation or a "Come to Jesus" meeting with that person and require each to be a contributor and not just a withdrawer! As a teacher, each of us must be an independent team player. If a teacher never contributes, but can execute a phenomenal lesson from your plan, that teacher needs to be taught how to contribute. Remember that part about strengths and weaknesses? Writing lesson plans may be that teacher's weakness. With guidance, support, and compassion, that weakness can grow stronger. You just don't want to burn out as a beginning teacher.

Speaking of burnout, take time for yourself! Teaching is your career and not your life. Never neglect family, friends, or your life for your career. Be present for your family as well as your students. When you are with your class, be there physically, mentally, and emotionally for your students. When you are home, be present physically, mentally, and emotionally for your family.

One of the last things that I want to tell you is to always behave in class the way you would if your administrator, central office personnel, or a parent is standing in your room. Say and do things that you can justify as being a strength for your students. If you screw it up, immediately find a way to fix it. Remember, you are human and you will make mistakes. Some mistakes will be humongous and need a lot of fixing. Others will be so minute that no one will notice. Learn from them all.

This leads to my final thought. Always reflect on your lessons and everything that happens in your classroom. Reflection happens during and after a lesson. When you see that "deer in the headlights" glazed-over look in your students' eyes, you have lost them. Do not continue to beat the dead horse. Instead, immediately apply mouth-to-mouth, defibrillation, or heart pumps or some type of resuscitation to that lesson to bring it back to life. Do something unexpected such as start singing (even if you can't "tote a note in a bucket!"), burst into laughter, have everyone jump up and do some stretching or other exercise, start some random game. Any or all of these things will bring your students and your lesson back to life, and give you a moment to redirect your lesson. Bugs Bunny is my hero. Why? He taught me to "Think quick, Rabbit!", which taught me how to think of a quick way to get out of any sticky or uncomfortable situation. As a teacher, you must be able to think quickly on your feet and change things so you do not miss a beat in your lesson. Should you miss a beat, change the tempo or find a new song!

Students are watching and listening, even when you think they are not. So be very careful of what you say or do in the classroom and in public. Be careful of social media. What you post is NEVER private. Remember that your administrators, colleagues, parents, and students are on social media, too. Post only those things that you are not fearful or ashamed of them seeing or hearing about.

Teaching is an amazing career. If you love it, it will not seem like a job, but an amazing adventure. When you stop loving it, get out! If you stay and don't love it, you'll do damage to yourself and your students. If you don't like children, don't teach! If you love it and give it the best you have each day, you will be rewarded by a student who comes back one day to say "Thank you."

Best of the best to you!
Love, Kathy Drew, Your older, wiser, and more experienced Self

P.S. So, was the "Dear Me" greeting of this letter a salutation or an exclamation of distress?

The teacher who wrote the next letter also created a series of text messages to her younger self to share her advice in a format more familiar to today's novice teachers. The text message exchange between the teacher and herself as a first-year teacher is included just after her letter.

Dear Gina,

Hello, old friend! I haven't thought of you in a while. So, right now you're thinking you want to be a teacher. What a great career choice! As with any career, teaching has many benefits. However, there are just as many drawbacks as well. That is why teaching requires passion and dedication. Along with every celebration, a disappointment is right around the corner.

I bet you're excited about the schedule. I mean, who wouldn't be? The schedule seems awesome. As a teacher, you will never get bored with the same mundane tasks, as with other jobs. Every day is different. You work Monday through Friday, with every weekend off. Teachers get almost every holiday, all major holidays, and summers off. With this schedule, you will have the opportunity to spend time at home with your family, vacationing, or just doing nothing at all.

On the other hand, will you have enough time to get it all done? There is so much material that needs to be covered. On top of that, there are many interruptions to the day. For example, pictures, assemblies, clubs, and various programs. Furthermore, after working all day, you will be required to stay after school for long faculty meetings, parent–teacher conferences, planning, cleaning, and extracurricular activities for students. Even when you're at home, you will have school on your mind and your mind on your students. Since every minute and then some is taken up at school, you will have to bring home papers to grade, data to analyze, and lessons to plan.

At first, you will feel very secure in your teaching job. Right now, the teaching field is wide open. There will always be children to teach and jobs available. In many states, there is a teacher shortage, so districts are desperate for good, dedicated teachers.

Consequently, one day soon you will learn about the state's expectations regarding teacher accountability for student success, and you will begin to worry about your job security. School districts are focused on data. High-stakes testing is used to make so many decisions, including the proficiency of a teacher. If or when you don't make the "goal," you may be placed an action plan and put under the microscope to improve something that is out of your control. This is going to be very stressful, and it will almost break you. There are so many factors that play into student success. You will be expected to show the same proficiency with all students despite the student's health, his or her background, home life, experiences or lack of, disabilities, language, behavior, attendance or lack of, and most of all, the student's willingness to learn. In comparison, it is like a doctor being blamed for a patient's illness, even when the patient isn't willing to accept treatment.

I would also suggest getting to know your students as a student and as a person. This will be very important. In fact, all other things in the classroom rely on these relationships. These relationships can make or break a student, and sometimes you. If student–teacher relationships are not positive, learning will most definitely not take place. Students will look up to and admire you, even when they don't act like it. You will have the amazing opportunity to make a great impact on students' lives. From the very first day of school, students depend on you for many things. Positive relationships allow students to feel more safe and secure. The students who feel safe and secure are more likely to enjoy school and learn more than others.

On the other hand, getting to really know your students can sometimes break your heart. There will be times when you learn things about your students that you don't want to know. Students will reveal information about a harsh home environment, use of drugs and/or alcohol, abuse, mental illness in the home, hunger and homelessness, and this can lead to a teacher "feeling sorry" for a child and not holding him or her to the usual high expectations. Although you may think you are making it easier on the student, you will actually be cheating the child out of the education he or she deserves.

One of the greatest benefits to look forward to is seeing your students learn and grow. The difference of a student at the beginning of the year and at the end of the year is unbelievable. They grow academically, socially, and emotionally. It's an honor to witness such important times in another life. You will be amazed!

Sometimes you will experience great disappointment when students do not grow. Some students will work as hard as they can and make very little progress. It will be heartbreaking to watch them fail time after time and finally give up on themselves.

Overall, teaching is like a bad drug. Once you experience the joy of sharing success with children, you can't go back. The glow that they get, the smiles on their faces when they finally accomplish something they've been working on— you can't get that anywhere else. The highs, the lows, the smiles, the tears. One day you may be "high" all day, and the next can be the worst hangover you've ever had. But, that high is worth it all . . . it leaves you "Jones-ing" for more. As for me, I chose teaching for the money and the fame.

Sincerely yours,
Yourself, 20-year Veteran, 3 times nominated, and 1-time Teacher of the Year!
(Gina Simmons)

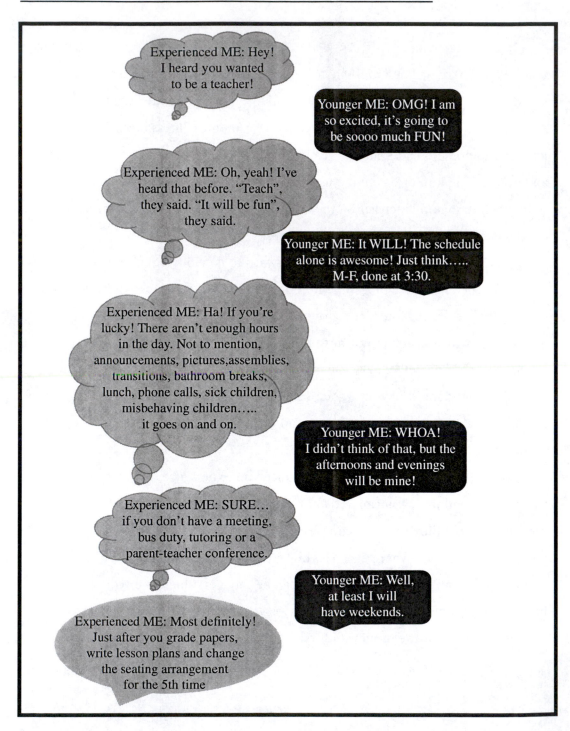

Younger ME: Yeah, but think of the job security. There will always be teaching jobs.

Experienced ME: TRUE. Until…….your students don't meet expected growth and you're placed on an action plan?

Younger ME: An Action Plan? How can I be put on an action plan if my students don't want to learn?

Experienced ME: My friend, regardless of what the student want to do, their abilities and disabilities, their health, home life and their attendance……. they still have a goal to meet and it's all on you girlie!

Younger ME: But…. But…. But….the kids will love me and I will love all of them.

Experienced ME: BAHAHAHAHAHAHAH! All of them will not love you and you certainly will not love all of them. But, the trick is to never let them know.

Younger ME: WOW! I'm getting a little anxious now!

Experienced ME: Don't be! You're here now, and you will love it. You will establish relationships that last a lifetime. You will impact lives every day. There will be tears and sometimes they will be your tears. Nothing will ever compare to the feeling you feel when you "see" when a student finally gets it, or when you've had all you can and a student slips you a note of encouragement. AND….the best part is the MONEY and FAME!

Kathleen,

Your mission, should you choose to accept it, is educating the third grade students at your school. Instructions will follow. This letter will self-destruct upon retirement from the school system.

What a fantastic and rewarding choice you have made! Educating children will give a new meaning to the word "life." As you begin your journey, let me give you some thoughts, tricks, and, perhaps, wisdom that I have gained.

1. Never doubt yourself or your ability to teach. There will be times, especially when all of your students do poorly on a test, that you question your abilities. This is a perfect time for you to reflect upon your teaching practices and lesson planning. You will find that you can restructure what the students did not comprehend and find success in a new way.

2. Utilize your mentor for everything—asking questions, setting up your room, preparing for parent–teacher conferences, ending the school year, and anything that might concern you about your students, yourself, or the school. Your mentor is a good sounding board that you will treasure on extremely tough days. You will have your mentor only for a short time, but you will treasure him or her forever.

3. Stand firmly planted and do not deviate from your rules, procedures, or consequences. During the first two weeks, plant the seeds of good behavior in your students. You must practice, practice, practice, and continue to practice what you expect of your students in order for them to grow. Difficulties with poor behavior and nonconformity to rules will be your downfall, if you falter from your stance.

4. Accept all of the children for who they may be. Learn about them. Visit their homes to see where and how they live. Then, when a child falls asleep in class or arrives out of sorts, it might make sense and allow you to handle the child in a different fashion. Realize, too, that these children need you to accept and love them as if they were your own. Make them feel safe and comfortable in their environment. Not every child wants to be at school. It is your job, as their teacher, to make them want to come. This might entail providing rewards, or just offering the satisfaction that the class will be the best in the entire school. Be sure that each child feels special and is told he or she is smart. Setting expectations extremely high will yield great results for you.

5. Be prepared and ready to teach your lessons. Your lessons should always revolve around your students' learning styles. Incorporate into every lesson a visual aid or a manipulative or a graphic organizer, perhaps one of the students' construction. If you are not prepared, your students will not learn. Lessons unprepared on paper do not turn out the way your brain might have thought they would.

6. Get your parents and community involved in your class. If you have stay-at-home moms or dads or parents who work second shift, invite them to assist in your room. They are more than willing to help. It also provides a connection among the parents, students, and you. If a parent cannot volunteer, permit the student to take home a camera. A digital camera can bring a student's family and life to class. Involving parents and the community creates a great team atmosphere in your classroom.

7. Become a part of the team at your school. The teachers in your grade level can help acquaint you with the procedures for your grade. Another important

part of the school team is the front office staff. They are vital to ensure the smooth running of the school and its success. Make sure that you get to know what they expect from you.

8. Although you have accepted a position teaching in a gateway grade, do not let the test be your guide to teaching. Integrate science, social studies, technology, language arts, reading, and math. This can be done, but it requires that you do some research and planning. Students need to learn the entire curriculum, not just reading and math for the test. If you are concerned about your students' success, then you have not taught the curriculum. Try to incorporate the necessary skills into games the students can play. If you have done your job all year, success will be yours.

9. Make learning fun. This does not mean playing and having a party. It means taking the time to make the students accountable for what they learn. They should be invited to be a part of the planning process. Ask questions to determine your students' interests. Most areas of student interest will fall within the curriculum. It is up to you to creatively address their interests in units that are designed to enrich their learning experiences.

10. Identify students who might be at risk during the first few weeks of school. Be sure to prepare the appropriate Personalized Education Plan (PEP), outlining how you will differentiate instruction for them. Many of your at-risk students will be on free and reduced lunch or economically disadvantaged. By targeting these students early, you will be in a better position to ensure that the students meet the requirements to move to the next grade. Along with identifying students at risk and preparing the necessary PEPs, you will also need to differentiate instruction

for students who are academically gifted. Sometimes this area is harder to handle. Differentiated instruction does not mean that you give the smart kids more work. It requires you to give these students more challenging work through higher-level thinking. Academically gifted students also have Individual Education Plans (IEPs), which require you to delineate exactly how you plan to differentiate the student's education to meet his or her needs.

11. Don't beat yourself over the head when deciding whether to retain a student. Try talking with the student about the chance to remain in the same grade another year to better a skill with which he or she is having difficulties. Remind the student of all the good qualities and abilities he or she has. You will be glad that you included the student in the decision. Sometimes students will want to remain in the grade a second time but are unable to voice this to you. Be sure to let them know you will be looking for their successes next year.

12. Be yourself! Your principal hired you, not someone else. Your principal is confident in your success, and you should be, too. If you have difficulties with your students or are feeling indifferent, talk to your principal. Your principal should be there to back you up all the way.

13. Always continue to learn. Professional development is an important part of your learning as a teacher. Be sure to include areas that might be of concern to you in your plans for development. Seminars and educational programs are offered to assist you in your quest to be the best you can be.

If you only remember one thing from this letter, let it be this: Just because you are new, this does not mean that you are not just as effective as a teacher who has been teaching for 30 years. The experiences you have brought to your classroom and school are valuable tools everyone can learn from. Have a fantastic first year!

Fondly,
Kathleen Wilderman
Always Striving to Know More!

Dear Newbie,

I blinked my eyes and 11 years have passed since I first began teaching. I still remember the excitement of having my very first classroom to decorate the day before Thanksgiving, having finished my student teaching requirement the previous day. I remember realizing the day after Thanksgiving break that I did not have any teacher manuals and that my students had to teach me what they had already learned that year with a sub. I, like my students, had SO much yet to learn!

I write to you today in the hopes that you will take my wise counsel and become a better teacher in the future. The field of education has changed drastically since that first panicked day of working with students. I have made many mistakes and had many triumphs. The blessing is that I have had the opportunity to start over each year with a different group of students and to make sure that I do not repeat my mistakes. Each day is a gift. I have accomplished more than I ever thought I would in the classroom. My methods of teaching have changed as I have kept up with and weighed the value of the most recent fads in the education world. Always take into consideration whether or not the latest teaching ideas are best for your students and your instructional goals.

Develop strong connections with your teammates and your mentor. They are your lifeline when you need help. On that note, don't be afraid to ask for help from your teammates, and in turn, to help them. Respect your next door neighbors and do not ignore them. Say "hello" and "goodbye." Respect their need for space or to talk. If you have a microwave in the office, refrain from warming up stinky food. You do not want your classroom to smell like fish all afternoon. Constantly watch those around you and learn from them. The best way to improve yourself is to learn from those around you. Ask questions, make suggestions, take constructive criticism to heart. If you can take this criticism well, you can keep growing as a teacher and avoid conflicts. Listen to your teammates. They know you better than you think.

Do not get pulled into the drama of the profession. Maintain an air of professionalism at all times. Speak about others in a positive way. Look for ways to be helpful at all times. This will make you a much happier, less self-centered person.

Make connections and network with teachers from other grade levels, from other schools, and in other counties. You never know when these connections will come in handy. Make your Professional Learning Network grow beyond your building. I have been hired for new teaching positions based on my reputation, my resume, and by knowing people at the new school. It is all about who you know! Make the effort to go to professional development workshops, even if they are scheduled on the occasional Saturday. It can only help you in the long run.

Excellent teachers constantly refine their craft. They do not put everything in a binder to use year after year. Do not spend your time reorganizing files every year. As you know, when I first began teaching, we did not use laptops or electronic devices. I wasted hours transitioning from folders, to binders, to different kinds of folders, and ultimately to digital resources. Slide it all in a paper or digital file and revise things for next year. Take notes on what worked and what did not. If you are working with electronic devices or files, fix the problems when you find them. You will never remember to do it next year. Always look for ways to make sure that your lessons are improving. Constantly repeating yourself makes you bored and ineffective.

Do not discount your favorite or least favorite subjects. I know you currently dislike science and social studies, but in the future you may find yourself teaching these subjects all day, every day, and you will love it! As a beginning teacher, I was asked to plan science for our grade level. I forced myself to spend time with it and developed a love for teaching in a hands-on way.

Listen to your administration. If they decide to move you to a different grade level, it may be because they see something inside of you that you don't see. Be willing to go with the flow. Take changes in teaching assignments as a challenge, not a punishment. Be flexible! I remember being told that I was moving from fifth grade to third grade. I initially viewed it as a punishment. Now, I see it as the best thing that has ever happened to my teaching career! I adore third grade, but did not realize that I needed to change grade levels to find this love. I repeat: Be willing to go with the flow!

Your first three years of teaching will not define you. They will also not be anything like your next ten years. Keep going. In the same way, do not let one bad year get to you. It won't break you. It will only make you stronger.

Look for ways to lead. Actively pursue ways to become a better teacher. Continuously try to refine your craft. Confer with other teachers, constantly read books, modify lesson plans, etc. And, when it becomes available, check with other teachers through social media for good ideas to incorporate into your teaching.

Find ways to make the learning connect to a real-life situation and/or job. Your goal in teaching should be to prepare your students for real life, not just a test. Genuine activities are more memorable. Kids LOVE to learn about real-life events like the Titanic. It only took me 11 years to realize that I could connect my entire motion and design unit in science to this event, and by doing so, the kids were eating out of my hand! Create ways to inspire and cause students to remember your class their entire lives.

The last bit of advice I have for you is to constantly add ideas for classroom discipline to your tool box. One classroom management system will not work for every child, every year of your career. Be prepared to modify your approach as needed.

Let me finish my letter by saying that TEACHING IS DEFINITELY WORTH IT! Be passionate about your career, and you will do well! You have many exciting years of teaching ahead of you!

Sincerely,
Megan Charlton

Dear Protector of Our Future,

I am writing this letter to you because I have had many years to reflect upon successes and failures throughout my career. Today, as a seasoned teacher of 13 successful years, I have gained some wisdom that I would like to pass on to you. In other words, I am offering you my gift of experiences. As an educator, your mission is to nurture, to educate, and to challenge students. You must create a loving, learning environment. You must deliver knowledge that addresses students' areas of weaknesses. You must engage students' minds, so that they meet their individual learning potential.

My four years of college didn't prepare me for what I encountered when I started teaching. College prepared me to teach children who were hungry for knowledge.

College did not prepare me for children who were physically hungry. Before you can teach a child, you must take care of their physical and emotional needs. If a child didn't eat dinner the previous night, it's your job to make sure those needs are met first. If a child is being abused at home, whether physically or mentally, it's your job to recognize those signs and seek necessary help. You may be the only advocate a child has. College prepared me to write lesson plans and to deliver instruction. College didn't prepare me to be a doctor, a nurse, a parent, a lawyer, or a psychologist.

You must create an environment in your classroom where children feel welcomed and loved. Children learn best in a safe and loving environment. A loving teacher doesn't necessarily tell his or her children that he or she loves them, but the message of LOVE is conveyed through his or her actions and tone. Children must feel that you genuinely care for them. If a child builds a bond with you, then teaching that child will be easy. Children naturally want to please the people they love. Always encourage and praise your children when they do something right. Recently, I had the unfortunate experience of dealing with the loss of a former student. He was 12 years old and was killed in a hunting accident. When I heard the news, I thought back to the last time I saw him and whether or not I left him on a positive note. Thank God, it was positive. As the day ends, make sure that you tell each child something positive. It's your job to build real relationships with the parents and the children.

Support will be essential to you as a beginning teacher. Don't be afraid to ask questions and seek out experienced teachers who are well respected in your school. Remember to stay away from teachers who are negative, because they will bring your energy down. Positive veteran teachers and administrators feel privileged to share ideas with new teachers. Please remember, you are not alone. I know that you don't want your administrator or other staff members to think that you need help, but he or she will be a wonderful asset to you. One more important point: Always create positive relationships with the secretaries, custodians, and cafeteria workers.

Caroline, remember that being prepared and organized will be crucial to your success as a teacher. A good start at the beginning of the year can be the difference between a great year and a year of disaster. Your plans should include plenty of meaningful activities that are fun for children and for you. Always remember to over-plan. If you don't plan adequately, your class will see you unprepared. It's always a good idea to keep folders of your lesson plans and activities. You will always be able to adapt your plans each year and make them better. Being unprepared leads to your students being bored, and discipline problems will result. It is wise for you set high expectations for your class. This does not mean each child has the same expectations. Each child is an individual, and it's your job to find out where that child is academically. You must challenge each child at his or her individual level. In your classroom, take on the role of a facilitator rather than a lecturer at times. Don't listen to teachers who tell you to teach to the middle, because you will lose the top and the bottom of your class. You are a lifetime learner, and truly effective teachers adapt and change with children.

You need to keep a professional journal so that you can reflect on your practices at the end of each day. Also, take pictures of your class and keep a photo album of all the fun activities you have provided for your children. A photo album is another way to reflect, and it's nice to share with your students. Children love to look through your photos and see their family members. I bet if I stay in this profession long enough, someone will see his or her mom or dad in those photos.

The last bit of advice that I'd like to offer encompasses your whole self. You must take care of yourself emotionally, socially, mentally, and physically. If you are tired and bogged down by paperwork, you can't make a difference in the lives of your students. Sometimes you'll feel like teaching isn't worth it, but I know that it is. It's all worth it when Ronnie, who is a senior, comes back to you with a book that you gave him as a second grader and tells you what a difference you made in his life. However, you need to read, go shopping, go to the beach, travel, have drinks with your girlfriends, spend time with your family, go to the gym, and take a mental health day every once in a while. Hang in there . . . You'll be great!

PS. I read something once that I feel that all teachers need to remember: "We can't wait for the storm to blow over. We have to learn how to work in the rain."

Love,
Caroline Locklear-O'Briant

This writer utilized a poem as his vehicle for communicating to his younger self some critical advice worthy of taking to heart.

Hello, My Younger Self

Hello, my friend
Long time no see
Please take some helpful advice
I know your circumstances intimately

You already work twelve-hour days

And weekends too

Creating some bomb lessons from scratch

Even your professors would agree that's true

Then you are told

About three new initiatives you will roll out

You have reservations

But do so with fidelity and no sign of a pout

To handle the increased load

You up your work hours

Often forget to call home

Your marriage nearly sours

You ignore those around you

They complain, "We've tried this before."

You go on like a good soldier

Only to find a drop in test scores

"What went wrong?"

You may ask

Listen carefully

For me, this is the past

The most important thing

Aside from your family, including a future daughter

Is educating your students

Don't get caught up in the fodder

You know your students well

You are reflective and seek improvement

Trust your expertise

If it improves learning, use it, otherwise lose it

That's not to say don't grow

Or explore

But don't be afraid to break the mold

Modify, adapt, question more

I hope those suggestions are helpful

To you and any readers to be

Don't forget to care for your world outside of work

Your future self appreciates these things

With high hopes that you'll heed this advice,

Your future and wiser self, Kenneth Hiroshige

Hey girl!

    I know you're busy, so I won't take up too much of your time. I hope you are taking care of yourself. As our ancestors and our dean of education taught us, "Before you can love others, you must first learn to love yourself." She modeled for us how important it is to eat well, exercise, and get plenty of sleep because little children take a lot out of you. I know how you are . . . Your abundance of energy often leads you to neglect yourself, thereby leaving your resistance low and not able to ward off small-children germs. (Smile) Stay healthy! You won't be able to enjoy teaching if you are working while ill.

    There are so many experiences and life lessons that I can share with you, but I will only focus on the few that I think will help you to become the excellent teacher that you want to be. Although you excelled in your undergraduate studies, you are now a *continually developing professional.* So this means you have to stay current with all the new developments in the field of early childhood. Would you have thought that we could finally have a degree and license in Zero to Three and Birth to Kindergarten education? It took a lot of research in special education and cross-cultural child development to bring about a paradigm shift in how we view young children. No longer do we think that infants primarily develop once they are born. We now know how early infants develop— cognitively—and how they are affected by sounds, pain, and the mother's stress hormones. Brain research and magnetic resonance imagining are a couple of the reasons we have been able to make such significant advances in our field. If you like, I can send you some of the research articles that I use in the university classes that I teach now. I managed to "stay current" by joining the Society for Research in Child Development, the National Council on Family Relations, and the National Association for the Education of Young Children. Not only did I join these professional organizations, I also read the publications and attended the annual meetings/conferences.

Some discussions are hard to have, but you will need to engage in them. Diversity is a very empty concept if we don't actualize our moments with each other to discuss issues of ethnicity (some call it race), class (especially poverty), and gender (LGBTQ), particularly when we are faced with disparities in these areas. For example, I no longer refer to parents because I know that children may be *parented* by someone who may or may not have birthed them or with whom they share genes and chromosomes. To honor that child and the child's *family* structure, I refer to *family* meetings, notes to *families*, open house for *families*. An important conversation to have with the child's family is the necessity (or not) of immunizations. Not everyone ascribes to the necessity of immunizations; it is sometimes connected to religious reasons. Also, I no longer assume the ethnicity of a child; they are encouraged to self-identify themselves. Diversity is diverse, indeed!

I know we have acknowledged the role of families and how important it is to respect them. It is even more important than ever. Family lifestyles and environments are changing. Not only are there "many worlds of childhood" as Urie Bronfenbrenner (1986) has said, but also the home-world is in flux. We have to make adjustments because many families don't have the same working hours as we do. My preprofessional students complain the most about "parents who don't come to school." They seldom consider that families are doing the best that they can, generally. I challenge them to consider ways in which families demonstrate that they care for and support their children. Once they see life through the lens of the families, they seek ways to be more flexible, like making phone calls, meeting them in different places, and being available at different times. We can't change the children's lives, but we can become more flexible, for the sake of the children, because they are focus of what we do—not us!

Oh! Do you remember that math class where you learned how to generate a FORTRAN program? *Well, the advances in technology never end!!!* You've got to keep up with *all* of it, or you will be left on the side of the road. It's everywhere and all of the time. Just smile and think about how you can always show something to someone else as you've learned something yourself.

And the Spanish that you thought you would never use again? *Guess what?* You'll do yourself a huge favor if you take a refresher course or two. While you're at it, a sign language course would make your life easier, too. Your classes will be much more diverse than you ever imagined. Given the way our paychecks are looking, you may want any extra income that you can manage as a translator.

As if all the preceding isn't important, I'd like to seriously impress upon you to consider the possibilities of administration. I know you LOVE the children and the hands-on aspect of education, but I *really* want you to think about administrative positions. Yes, "women hold up half the sky," but it isn't reflected in educational leadership roles. I don't think enough of us (females) are encouraged to become principals, superintendents, deans, or state lawmakers who care and focus on education platforms. We have to engage and participate in the educational system and institutions at every level. I can tell you that I thoroughly enjoyed my administrative positions because I was able to create programs, gain leadership skills, help others learn leadership skills, and promote best practices to a larger audience. Imagine being able to implement all you've learned in your undergraduate and graduate studies as a director of a public service center. You can do it! Just be open to that prospect, OK? Promise me?

I've got to go. I have several other meetings today: a webinar to help *improve my course* in health and safety; a student that I'm *mentoring*; and preparing a *presentation* with a colleague for a conference. Self-improvement, mentoring others, and sharing your practical knowledge with other professionals are constant in this profession. These are all the activities that I'm expecting you to do as your professional development increases. You can do it a little at a time, that is, incrementally. How do you devour a dinosaur, one of my instructors or mentors in my PhD program asked? The answer? One bite at a time.

I—well, I guess I should say "WE"—earned "OUR" PhD exactly like that … one bite at a time. Creating family came first. Then, as positions in kindergarten were scarce, I was encouraged by my former dean to earn a master's degree in special education. This led me to becoming a pediatric behavioral specialist and developing an interest in behavioral disorders, particularly child sexual abuse. I wanted to contribute to the development of the knowledge in that field, and the only way to do it was by creative research and practice. I "bloomed" in child and family development, and I believe I am a poster child for lifelong learning. My advice to you, my younger self, is this: Grab every opportunity that comes along to grow professionally!

I just wanted you to know that I was thinking about you and cheering your professional development. I saw a documentary about Maya Angelou on PBS last week, and it reminded me about your Senior Day at college. Remember how we spent a lot of time trying to find the theme for our class and who best expressed how we saw ourselves? You will recall that we found the poet, Gwendolyn Brooks (1968), and her legacy to us was:

For we are the last of the loud.

Nevertheless, live.

Conduct your blooming in the noise and whip of the whirlwind.

It was a whirlwind then, and it's a whirlwind now. Take care of yourself.

Always,
Frankie Denise Powell, PhD

References

Bronfenbrenner, U. (1986). Alienation and the four worlds of childhood. *The Phi Delta Kappan*, 67, 430–436.

Brooks, G. (1968). Second Sermon in the Warpland. In the Mecca: poems. Retrieved March 4, 2017 from https://betterblackness.wordpress.com/2014/01/01/the-second-sermon-on-the-warpland-by-gwendolyn-brooks/

Dear Self,

Congratulations! You earned your degree and now you are a teacher! But, I need to fill you in on something . . . The name, "*teacher*," is quite misleading. Your career choice, which others call "teacher," implies the work you will do is primarily to teach. In reality, teaching is a small portion of what you will do. Teaching is actually the easy part of the job. All of those classes that you just completed regarding curriculum, content, differentiation, and technology . . . Those are essential components, but let's talk about what you REALLY will be doing in this role of "teacher."

You will be a *listener*. Listen to children, parents, students, administration, and colleagues. With the information you receive, use discernment to filter, reflect, adjust, feel, analyze, and change daily. Listening may be the most important job in your first year. In your first year as a teacher, the principal will observe you, and the lesson will fall apart. You will be humiliated when she meets you in her office the next day. Instead of defending yourself or thinking about quitting, just listen. Reflect on the advice given, ask questions, and listen some more.

You will be a *connector*. Connect information so that it has meaning to the students. Ask your students, how a skill will help them in their future career? Connect yourself with each student in your class, the community, the families that you work for, the staff members within your building and district. Connecting doesn't happen on its own; you have to go out of your way to make it happen. Some students don't want to connect, because then they are vulnerable, and you can really make a change. These students are challenging, but find a way to connect with them. Connecting will feel uncomfortable because you are an introvert, but it will get easier for you as you continue teaching. You will realize that the connections that you have among teachers and within the district will lead to opportunities beyond anything you are capable of completing on your own.

You will be a *risk-taker*. Try, even when nobody else on the team will join you. Try writing grants. Interview for new positions when you know it is time for a change. Pay attention to your ideas, and follow through with those that deserve to be lived out.

You will be a *learner*. Learn the strengths, weakness, interests, passions, and stories of each student that walks through your door. Learn ways to follow the mandates of the district and state without compromising what is best for your students. Learn from veteran teachers. Learn from new teachers. Learn unconventional ways to teach standards so that complacency doesn't sneak into your classroom. Learn how to avoid negative voices as well as fixed mindsets.

You will be an *encourager*. Encourage children, parents, students, administration, and colleagues. Encourage students to try. Encourage parents to remember that you are a team and you are in this together. Encourage colleagues as they show up in spite of personal challenges or as they go through the general daily challenges in the classroom. You may be surprised to hear me say to encourage administration, but I have learned that they are part of your team. They want you to be successful, and encouraging them when appropriate builds the "team."

You will be a *problem solver*. Problem solve when the field trip doesn't go as expected. Problem solve when you analyze data and realize many students still haven't learned the information you taught. Problem solve when you are balancing the demands of teaching with the unexpected happenings of your family life.

You will be a *believer*. Believe that each child can learn. Believe that the work that you do daily helps the world. Believe that you can and will make it to June, Friday, or maybe even the end of the day. Believe that mindset is more important than skill, talent, or ability, both for yourself and your students.

You will be a *life-changer*. Change lives by providing opportunities to students that they never knew existed. Change lives by being the parent figure that some of your students have never known. Change lives by providing accommodations and support for students with special needs. Change lives by introducing students to their interests and passions. Change lives by looking students in the eyes and telling them they are important and have unique gifts.

So, *listener, connector, risk-taker, learner, encourager, problem solver, believer,* and *life-changer,* know that most will simply call you "*teacher*." You will meet an older gentleman who will look you in the eyes and unflinchingly, say

"You will be doing good to make it even a year as a teacher." Just hold your head high and know that you will make it well beyond a year. Yes, you are a "*teacher*," but you are SO MUCH MORE! You are amazing, and you make me proud!

Sincerely,
Your future self,
Katie Weed

December 19, 2016

Dear Teacher Adventurer,

It is with great honor that I have been asked to welcome you as you begin a new phase in your life! Welcome to your new career!

Do not enter without courage or desire to face new obstacles. Come with plans to succeed! There are hundreds of little "minds" waiting for educational experiences that only you and others who have entered with you and before you can give.

It is perfectly normal to be afraid, but do not let "THEM" smell your fear. They can, and will, pick up on any apprehensions that are apparent! You must be well versed in disguising the anxiety and apprehension that exist inside. We all face self-doubt from time to time. It is how we channel the struggle that makes us successful.

You must remember that it is you who are now the adult. Do not be surprised when they test your authority. It is how you establish your alpha position. Children want a strong and wise leader. They will recognize your confidence and respect it. Respect goes a long way on both sides of a teacher–student relationship. Show your students that you respect them by remaining in control!

Love them always, and no matter how much of a bath they might need! Find ways to meet their needs. It might not always be with actual things, but with words of encouragement and honesty.

Work to establish a relationship even with the students who seem hardest to win over. Kids work for people they think believe in them! Even the ones who are the nonstop talkers or the greatest of instigators, and/or bullies! Make them think they can be more than they are. Be honest and expect much! Your expectations might be the only ones they ever have to meet!

Remember that mistakes grow new neural paths (including the teacher's) and that every child has the ability to learn. They are not all alike! Just because the powers that be claim that they all should be able to add and subtract fractions with unlike denominators in fifth grade with only five days of good instruction, it doesn't necessarily mean that they will! The object of the game is to give them all the tools they need to make it to that goal, and to be sure they know that they are no less important if they don't "get it" right away!

Keep working and improving! You are also a work-in-progress. If at first you don't succeed! . . . Try something different. Don't think twice about asking the more experienced teachers how they get things done! Just because we might not wear the most current fashions or aren't up to date on the newest social media doesn't mean we haven't figured out how to get growth from the kids who are the hardest cases! None of us experienced teachers "knows" all the tricks! It's just that we have developed a nice tool kit of strategies for reaching every type of child that crosses the threshold of our rooms! We're a bit weathered and worn, but we have survived many changes in education. Find yourself someone who is willing to share, and use his or her practices to find your own teaching voice!

No one walks into a classroom as an expert. Be willing to ask for help and pay close attention to the teachers who are getting the job done! Be brave and vigilant! Thank you for picking up and carrying the torch because someday, you will need to hand it on to me, your future self!

Sincerely,
Sharyl Gross

Dear Younger Self,

How many times as a young kid did I hear "Readin', 'Ritin', and 'Rithmetic" was key? In reality, while those three "R's" are important, as content learning must take place, here are **four additional "R's"** that are just as vital. These are four concepts I wish I had paid as much attention to in my early days of teaching.

The first *R*: **RESEARCH**. H-m-m . . . Not technical research per se, but truly knowing the concepts that are important to school administration, school culture, and community. Research—truly know inside and out—what is important to your school administrators. He or she has experience that benefits everyone, even if you think at times he or she is an ineffective role model. Trust me, there is something valuable to be gleaned! More importantly, he or she knows what is important in regard to school law, content curriculum, and much more. It really is true that sometimes we just don't know what we don't know. Research what is important to the community, and value and honor it.

Secondly, **RECIPROCITY** certainly means to develop relationships— with students, peers, and the community—but it is so much more. Develop relationships, true relationships. Know your students and what is important to them. Investing in others keeps it real. Reciprocity is also learning to devote yourself to the well-being of others, especially when you don't necessarily feel like it. On days you want to quit, find someone to help, as there is always someone struggling more than you.

The third _R_, **REFLECTION**, is the hardest trait for anyone, because we have to admit there is room for growth and improvement. Probably the most freeing thing I have learned is the ability to say, "I was wrong, I made a mistake, and I apologize." As long as kids are not physically lost or hurt, the rest can be worked out. Set aside time every day to reflect. What could have been done differently, stated differently, or researched in order to improve? Just remember to take time to have fun along the way. Laugh each and every day; laugh with others and at yourself.

And finally, the fourth _R_: Be willing to **REINVENT** yourself, stay current. Being stagnant never adds dimension. Step out, reinvent yourself, be a risk-taker alongside your students. Start a positive movement. After all, isn't that the reason you started this journey to begin with?

Keep in mind these **four additional "R's"—RESEARCH, RECIPROCITY, REFLECTION, REINVENT**—every year throughout your teaching career. Doing so will help you to continuously grow in this wonderful profession of teaching. Enjoy the amazing journey you are commencing! One day, before you know it, you will look back through my eyes and see how important each of these four R's were to your success!

Gratefully yours,
Susanne Long

Dear Young Irene,

Congratulations on joining a difficult, but most rewarding, profession, and the profession of your beloved grandmother. The trick to effective teaching? No tricks, it's actually all **treats**, and I'm willing to share these with you to help you have a great start to your career. I believe these treats will enable you to better find your own teaching path among the endless routes available.

Treat every student with respect. Indeed, treat each as if they were the child of your most beloved friend, principal, or superintendent. Each child deserves the same respect as the other children, despite the family's socio-economic status, background, or attitude. Always remember that a child may have been through a personal tragedy, even that morning. A child may have just lost a loved one, witnessed a shooting, or experienced physical, mental, or emotional abuse. You may not know it, but one of them did. Also, they may just be having a bad day, and you are the one person that can turn the day around.

Treat your students to a safe classroom. Naturally, you will remove physical hazards, teach students how to carry scissors, monitor their movement, prevent arguments the best you can, but I'm talking about students being safe by being in a classroom where one is accepted and loved. Help your students learn to appreciate our differences and find the inner beauty of others. You need to open your mind to cultural, religious, and familial differences. Rather than turn up your nose when a student brings in a "strange" dish, realize that many foods common to your culture would seem foreign to others. If a child wears a burka and other students seem to find this odd, have the child share the history, background, or reasons for the clothing. Ask other students to share not-so-common items of clothing that may be in their family. Perhaps a uniform of someone in the military, regalia of Native Americans (there would be many types), the kimono, and obi. Make the experience an ongoing event where students bring in or describe interesting foods, places to live, and traditions. Discuss related history and geography as it relates to clothing, food, and materials. Create a learning experience where you and your students grow to appreciate differences and anxiously wait to learn something new, an experience they will remember long after they may have forgotten anything else from the year.

Treat your students' needs. Check to make sure they have had something to eat (usually provided by the school), and clothing (there is usually a clothing closet in the school or check with PTA, local churches, or Christian closets), but there are other areas you may not have considered. Services through your school will provide a student counseling, reading glasses, or a nurse's care, as well as function to meet many other needs. Check with your principal, make a list of available resources, and keep the list handy. Obviously, it is difficult for students to learn well if they are worried about meeting basic needs.

Treat your students to your advocacy. Address the needs mentioned above, but also "fight" for your students—the equipment they need, the experiences they desire, and the dreams they may possess. Go to the local school board, write a grant, or meet with parents. At this juncture in their life, you are the best chance your students have for a better future.

Treat each moment as the one moment you have to teach your students important content, not just take up time. Select supporting activities and materials that best convey the concept to the widest number of children. Truly check for understanding and reteach in a novel way that might assist anyone who did not understand the first teaching. Make it fun or interesting, but make it count. Optimize your teaching time by automatizing tasks. Don't call the roll, for example. Instead, have student pick up their name tag or move their clothespin to "present" when they enter the room. Always, always, always allow students to have a book at their desk or meaningful work to do if they finish and are waiting on others or there is some down time.

Treat each student as an individual, making sure one doesn't fall behind. You really are not teaching a class of students. You are teaching a classroom of individuals. Each moment of each day counts for each child, and your effort can make a difference.

Treat each concept as if it is fascinating and relevant to the students' futures beyond the idea that they will need the understanding to do next year's school work. How do you do this? You find out why it is important and how it relates to their lives (which involves knowing your students). Become interested in the topic yourself. To do this, conduct the research necessary to truly understand the concept, how to best teach the concept, the role the concept plays in the world, and how the concept can be useful to your students. You can become excited about how you are teaching the concept, even if the concept itself doesn't thrill you.

Treat your colleagues as if they know the answers to your problems, and show them the respect they deserve. Then consider their responses with a bit of skepticism. Do their suggestions support your philosophy of how to best treat and teach students? Does a particular suggestion match what research and your experiences determine to be best practices? Research their responses as if there is more to the story. See if you can improve the idea or find a better way.

Treat your actions as if someone is watching you, because they are. I remember distinctly watching the Health and PE teacher eat an ice cream for lunch. I remember when my fifth grade teacher encouraged me to share my comment on a girl's pretty dress. The girl had learning difficulties and was often ostracized by the rest of the class. I remember seeing my teacher help serve the community Thanksgiving dinner for the needy, and I remember when a teacher was arrested for a DUI. People expect more of a teacher. A teacher, even after work hours, is held to higher standards, and people do notice.

Treat your work as if it is not your whole life, because it isn't. It will be a big part of your life, and you will feel like you are almost always working, but make sure you are taking care to meet your own social, emotional, and physical needs, or you won't be much good for the students, and you will likely lose your zest for teaching.

Treat yourself to the wonders, the marvels that are your students. They will delight you, intrigue you, and bring you a satisfaction that is rarely experienced. If you allow them to, they will teach you more than you ever thought possible.

Sincerely,
Your 29-year-veteran self,
Irene Pittman Aiken

Dear Novice Teacher Sylvia,

It's normal to be apprehensive, intimidated, and even frightful of the unknown. But there's also that element of mystery that once you finally dive in and "bite the bullet," you'll think, "What was I so afraid of?" There's no blueprint that will map out every nuance you will encounter over the years, but just like your fingerprints that no one has but you, your students will carve a niche in your heart that's reserved only for you.

There's a world awaiting you that will be life changing because you're like Hallmark, you care enough to send the very best, and that's you, *Teacher*. Adapting to teaching will be second nature because nurturing for you is like breathing air. Teaching has beckoned you since childhood when, at the young age of 10, you helped care for your baby brother. First-year jitters will quickly pass as you envelop the curriculum and teach with abandon to your young charges. Your students will be your students in every sense of the word. Every year will be like going through the birthing process (not literally of course) in that there's new life and bonding that will last a lifetime. Even though you have four children of your own as you begin to teach, your body will need to adapt to the new environment where you will be closely housed with up to 29 students. The very first year, the flu will ravage your body like a thief entering your house uninvited. It's all part of the adapting process. Fortunately, though, it will pass.

As your students come, seeking knowledge, approval, guidance, acceptance, and love, they will not only gain those things, but they will leave their mark upon you. Early on in your career, you will establish yourself as the teacher who not only teaches, but takes care of the whole child. Taking care of the whole child equates to cleaning up throw-up, changing soiled clothes, cleaning cuts and scrapes, applying Band-Aids and cold compresses. And just because you will do things that aren't written under a teacher's responsibilities, don't think everybody else is going to do it. As a mother and a teacher, your nurturing nature is never off duty. Please take heart in knowing that your efforts to go beyond the call of duty will not go unnoticed, but will come back to you in more ways than one. But you won't do it for recognition. You'll do it because it's the right thing to do and because that's who you are.

As the years quickly pass by, you will reflect upon how much you have changed physically and how you've grown into a confident and outspoken advocate for children. While your outward appearance might change, the core of who you are is constant and unwavering. Your students will be with you wherever you go and occupy a place in your heart that is big enough to love the hundreds of students you will teach in your lifetime.

And it's good that you have a strong constitution because there will be days your heart will be so broken you won't think you'll be able to keep going. You will cry when you find out one of your students is being physically abused. But you will intervene and do what you need to do. While we never think about our students leaving this world before us, it does happen sometimes. You will cry and mourn the loss of "one of your babies." When your name is mentioned in the educational arena, your fellow colleagues and superiors will speak of you fondly.

Your summers will be spent getting rejuvenated for your new group of students. The secretary will let you know that the parent request list for your class filled up first. That will be a good thing because winning over the parents is part of the job. And it's also one of the greatest compliments because they will be entrusting you with the most precious thing they have. There will be those students who tug at your heart so much, you will want to take them home. And some of them, you will. As they sit at your feet looking upon you in awe, always remember that it's not what you might say, but your actions that they will remember long after they have left your class.

Some of the little girls you teach will wish you were their mama, while some of the little boys you teach will want to marry you. Yes, we're talking about kindergartners. You will treasure the handwritten notes, pictures, gifts, and other memorabilia you will receive over the years. You will also stay in the profession long enough to see some of your former students become teachers, too. You'll also have the privilege of teaching doctors, pharmacists, law enforcement officers, nurses, those in the armed forces, plumbers, electricians, and those who will end up on the wrong side of the law and become incarcerated.

Because of the love of your profession and a desire to afford your students the best methodologies of teaching, you will earn Masters in Elementary Education, and School Administration degrees. While you will spend many weekends with textbooks and computers as your constant companions, the knowledge you gain will transfer to your students. And you will also have the opportunity to meet so many wonderful people you will cherish and with whom you will build special relationships.

There will be evaluations, evaluators, and administrators that recognize your potential and will encourage you to go into school administration. As a devout teacher, you will reply with an adamant, "No." But you will want to become an advocate for teachers, and so you step outside your comfort zone. As a school administrator, you will not only continue to impact the lives of children on a grander scale, but teachers, too. It will come at a cost, though. Because of your heartfelt desire to do the right thing, it will mean that sometimes you will end up doing your job and somebody else's, too. But that short deviation will lead you back home where you embrace self-contained teaching all over again.

When it seems like the world is full of craziness, you'll step into your room and look into the faces of your students, and the innocence in their faces will make you forget about what's happening on the outside because you need to be in the present for your students. They will love you with an innocence of purity.

And at home, parents often will hear, "My teacher said..." Please remember that everything you do and say is being absorbed by them. Your likes, dislikes, mannerisms, beliefs, and tolerance will greatly impact their lives. And after 30 years have lapsed, one of your own children will call and say, "Mama, I saw one of your former students today. She said, 'You must be Ms. Sylvia's daughter.'" And your husband will say, "Can we go anywhere that you don't know somebody?" Going to the grocery store or other retail stores will usually end in a family reunion of former parents or students. And you will love hearing the words, "You haven't aged any."

While this letter might give you a glimpse of some of the best years of your life, there are so many other things that are awaiting you that words will not adequately prepare you for. As you wake each day and pray for discernment, take heart in knowing that teaching is the profession that paves the way for all other professions. Your name may never appear on a marque, but it will be embedded in the hearts and minds of the greatest resource we have, and that's *our children*.

From YOU speaking from the distant future,
Always cheering you on,
Sylvia Averette

Wide-Eyed, Eager Mr. Plummer,

As you step over the threshold of your first, bare-walled classroom, your smirk-faced whisper is barely audible. Your thought is shared with only your own ears and the mismatched, hand-me-down furniture stacked haphazardly in the corner. *"This is where I will spend the next 30 years of my life."* You have but only a few weeks to transform this barren desert into the innovative, creative, life-changing machine you have only had visions of in your dreams. While your days with students still linger in the distance, your challenge of learning your way through this thing called "*TEACHER*" has just begun. Listen carefully, think critically, and act responsibly.

Hold tightly to your values of learning. A framed degree hangs proudly on a nail, but it does not, however, give you omniscient powers for solving the problems of the world. You were first a learner, and you should forever strive to absorb and continue to grow. Each and every experience from this moment forward is an opportunity to build a knowledge base of all that is important to your success. Potential for self-education lurks in every hallway, hides under every cafeteria table, sticks between the pages of every book, and masks itself behind every closed door. Always have an open eye, searching for ways to satisfy your professional curiosities and foster your development as a teacher. Lean on experienced mentors in the building; never be afraid to admit your faults, your mistakes, your "I have no idea what to do!" feelings. Read professional literature to keep abreast of modern trends and research-based strategies being implemented to reach optimal achievement. Simply using trendy "buzz words" is not enough; yearn to be the resident expert on the latest high-yield practices. Connect with teachers around the world who are equally as inspired to change tomorrows. You are but a speck in this world of innumerable possibilities.

Be the hand that first reaches out to shake another. Relationships are the universal foundation for success and stand as the strongest power to enable connection. One bright smile, the simplest "*Good morning!*" or a hand-written note of thanks or praise can ignite the grandest repercussions of positivity and offer benefits of contagious gratitude for years to come.

Extend your abilities and talents to support others' needs throughout the school; others—especially the secretary and custodians—will look after you if you show them the same respect. It may be as trivial as creating routines for your students to deliver yearbook money promptly to the office and to clear the floor of pencils and scraps of paper each day before lunch, but the smallest actions often mean the most—even if it only earns a slice of pie when the local church drops off a dessert in the office or a classroom that gets vacuumed four days this week when the others are vacuumed only three. Do not join in the gossip circles and the drama of the school community; if they are talking behind others' backs, they are doing the same to you when you are not present. Parents hear the "he said, she said" comments, but they are truly only concerned with your interest in their children. Parental relationships are grounded in your desire for discovering a child's best and understanding your role in supporting his or her weaknesses. The best children are not kept at home, while the worst are sent to school each day. Parents send you all they have. Their expectation is that you build the same strength with their children, so strong you are viewed as "hero" in their young eyes.

Never lose sight of your true purpose. In every situation that presents itself, put your students first. It becomes all-too-easy to use the references "*my* classroom, *my* books, *my* schedule, *my* class," for example, but are *you* the real reason each of those exists? Purposely change your language to reflect *our* real priorities—the students, their learning, and their futures. As you prepare and plan for instructional rigor, consider what is best for the children. Ask yourself, "What do *they* need? What do *they* enjoy? Ultimately, what have *they* learned?" School is not as much about *you* as you once thought it was. Instill essential principles in hearts and minds of your students that will be necessary and last a lifetime. You yourself may enjoy the holiday season, but how will a future 30-year-old really thrive knowing a little more about the German Santa Claus in your "Christmas around the World" unit? And, Johnny Appleseed? Month-long studies of him do not produce rocket scientists! You hold your students' hands as they take their first steps into the unknown. Make it meaningful. Make it count.

Step outside your comfort zone. Education, just as much as anything in today's society, is ever-changing. No two days, no two students are alike. Be confident in your dedication and desire to do what is best for every child who enters the classroom. It is never enough to simply think outside the box; instead, always be prepared to recreate the box. The possibilities are endless, and "too much, too far" does not exist. Problem-solve concerns and make adjustments to reach solutions until you arrive at the desired outcome. While you may be the "new kid on the block," it does not mean you are bound by the traditional ways your experienced counterparts have always "done" school. Play around with the layout and atmosphere of the classroom to maintain students' curiosity and to indulge their interests. Break up instructional blocks of time to best suit their abilities and attention spans. Stop for instructional brain breaks; trick them into thinking they are only playing. Use every minute, bell-to-bell, as an opportunity to teach. Never stand stagnant waiting for the restroom. Invite students to sit with you at lunch for book talks. Keep flashcards handy in your back pocket at all times. Fresh, new ideas engage brain activity and leave children with a hunger for more. Imagine the excitement created when they are the experts teaching their peers, when they are the ones doing the majority of the talking, when they are ones determining how they are assessing and proving their own mastery. Children will rise to the expectations you set for them.

A student-led, teacher-facilitated classroom operates best as a well-oiled machine through the guise of organization. Everything in the classroom should have a place, and everything with a place should hold a purpose. Much of life is experienced through chaos, especially in the fast-paced mind of a child. Allow structure to be a cone of safety, an environment in which expected routines thrive and practical procedures dictate collaboration and interaction. Develop a system for what holds true, instructional merit, while purging outdated or irrelevant resources of little value. Students deserve to be presented with the most current information and strategies, not always a store-bought poster left by your predecessor and purchased in 1996. Instruction beginning with this type of content often leads to a lesson merely *covered*, only "teaching" it because the standards told you to. Teaching students to investigate beyond surface level knowledge requires a great deal of organizational planning from day one. Know your content. Organize the year to seamlessly integrate content to scaffold students' understanding. Embrace each new year as a reason to review what you have done to make greater strides and gains, reorganizing your own thoughts to prepare for a new year of challenges.

Within your thoughts lies an abundance of power never to be dismissed. The benefits of reflection are immeasurable and, without doubt, the path to further success. Take time each day to contemplate what has been given to you, and what you have given to others. We make good choices, and we make bad choices. The true spirit of teaching comes alive as we interpret these choices and how we then choose to act and react to them. Take your thoughts a step further; put your words on paper. Set aside a time—even five minutes each day—to journal about your adventures. Let out your frustrations. Describe obstacles students overcame. Share your thoughts on particular lessons and restrategize methods for better teaching the lesson next time. Jot down ideas for resources. Dream about the perfect classroom setup. Make this written exposition completely about you and becoming your best. Revisit your journaling from time-to-time, but make a commitment to add to your thoughts, as the days, months, even years, progress. The stories you think you will always remember; you certainly will not. The craziest of days will soon be overshadowed by your most exciting journey yet.

Teachers spend so much time simply thinking of others that they often forget to take the time to breathe and be a cheerleader. Celebrate students. Celebrate success. Celebrate yourself. Every new day is filled with tiny milestones worthy of a little cheer. Spread the joy of learning and make it contagious both within your classroom and throughout your school. Opportunities for celebration are constantly around us and only motivate us to reproduce those successes and reciprocate those emotions. Make the most of every moment, finding every reason possible to make someone smile and feel good about himself or herself, and ultimately, make this world a better place. No one does it like you!

No one ever promised this career to be easy, but 12 years down the road, I promise you will look back and wonder where the time has gone. While you continue to expand your own insights of teaching, the interpersonal connections you have made along the way are what truly bind your love for learning. Even outside your comfort zone, students come first and will exceed expectations in your organized chaos. May you always look forward, remembering the past, and celebrating all that is yet to come. No, Mr. Plummer, you may not physically spend the next 30 years in that first, bare-walled classroom, but one thing is certain. *A love for teaching will spend a lifetime in the same place—deep in your heart!*

Embracing every tomorrow with experience and reflection,

Mr. Lynn Plummer II, M.S.A.

Letters Written to Novice Middle and Secondary Level Educators

"The greatest thing is, at any moment, to be willing to give up who we are in order to become all that we can be."

Max De Pree (1924–__), American businessman and writer, author of <u>Leadership is an Art</u> *(1987).*

Salutations Fatos,

Welcome to the wonderful world of teaching. As a new teacher, it is a frightening thought that students will depend upon you to learn. I am here to help you through the transition into the teaching field with some words of advice and wisdom. There are three key areas that I think would benefit you the most: *classroom management*, *differentiated instruction*, and *flexibility*. If you get these key factors down your first year, then you will be on the road to being not only a successful teacher, but also starting to enjoy your job.

The first topic I want to cover is *classroom management*. As a first-year teacher in middle school, you have to start on behaviors from the very first day. Middle school students have been in school for a long time; they know the rules. They are deciding what kind of teacher you are and what they can get by within your room. Students say they want a nice and relaxed teacher, but what they really want is a consistent and firm teacher. Students want to know what they can expect from you with homework, class work, grading, and how you handle classroom behaviors. Students do not want to get picked on or bullied, and they expect you, as the teacher, to handle these situations. You should handle any unwanted behaviors in the classroom swiftly and consistently. This does not mean to address every behavior; you have to choose your battles.

A couple of behavioral situation examples might be helpful to you. If a student challenges your authority, see the student outside of the classroom. This takes away the audience and frequently de-escalates the situation rapidly. Always try to use the parents; don't be afraid to call them. Parents are useful allies and will help you with their child and will frequently end many behavior problems quickly. Also, you must keep the students busy. Downtime often leads to socializing and problems.

Some strategies that didn't work were making threats, using reflective sheets, or being too nice. Threats don't work unless you follow through with them and unless you are consistent with everyone. Students will complete "reflective" sheets, designed to make them think about what they did and why, as much as you want, and then just continue misbehaving. Being too nice didn't work either; even the best students will try to take advantage of the situation.

The second piece of advice as a new teacher is on handling *differentiated instruction*. It is easy to think that everyone learns the way we do, but that is just not the case. You need to research different ways of teaching information. There are books, Internet websites, school materials, and other teachers. Use all of your resources and observe other teachers during your lesson planning. This always gave me some good ideas to use in my classroom. I had to observe another teacher in my first year, and she was using a Jeopardy-themed review game with her students before a test. I thought this was a brilliant idea!

I also found that using my special education teachers for ideas to meet the needs of my special education students was very helpful. Although you are teaching social studies, and students do not get additional support for social studies classes, I was stunned to find that some of my students could barely read at a second grade level. I had to work really hard at including them in projects and activities without bringing their reading problems to everyone's attention. I found that talking to the special education teachers that serve those students really was helpful in differentiating my instruction; they are a great resource.

My last piece of advice is to realize the importance of *flexibility*. Planning your lessons for a week or several weeks is great, but you must learn to be flexible. In the school, many activities throw off your schedule. Sometimes it is a fire drill, meeting, activity in the auditorium, or just not getting to work at the pace you would like. It helps to be creative and think on your feet, which you can't always plan for ahead of time. Sometimes these are my best lessons or activities for the students.

As a final thought for your first year, try not to get overwhelmed with paperwork. When I first thought about teaching, I only thought of lesson planning, teaching, and grading. I had no idea that there was so much more, like participating on committees, using Edmodo, having a duty at sporting events, making a professional development plan, interventions for students, team planning, and integrating international themes into my lessons. There are so many extras that it can become overwhelming. There is a whole new world of paperwork to complete when you are a teacher. I had no idea that they had so many forms to fill out and child information to keep track of every day. To be quite honest, I find it to be repetitive at times, and I really felt overwhelmed at first. My advice is not to panic and just ask for help. Every teacher in your school has been a first-year teacher at one time, and many of them know how it feels.

So if you take the whole paperwork and planning piece in a relaxed manner, if you get your classroom under control, and if you continue to develop your teaching strategies, you will have a successful first year. Of course, all year you will feel really behind and overwhelmed, which is perfectly normal. But by the end of your first year, you will feel like you are getting the whole system down, and you will be ready for a much needed break. Just remember: don't try to be perfect; it won't happen and nobody expects you to be.

Have a Great First Year!

Your Future Self
Fatos Fanaj

December 1, 1981

Dear Laura,

You're not even halfway through your first year of teaching sixth grade, yet you are very discouraged. Each day you drag yourself to school, hating the thought of walking into that classroom and wondering if you'll survive the school year. People tell you that the first year is the most challenging and next year will be so much better, but you wonder if you can even make it to the end of the day. Your students are often rude and disrespectful, and teaching isn't turning out to be what you thought.

Well, I'm here to encourage you to stick it out for the rest of the year. One day, you'll be glad that you stayed in the teaching profession. Who am I? I am a voice from your future; I'm the teacher that you will be one day, 23 years from now! I'm traveling through time to offer you advice and encouragement, to make sure that you don't make the biggest mistake of your life by giving up the profession you chose many years ago.

Before I share some advice about how to survive your first year, I'd like you to take a mind journey with me to the future. Perhaps it would help you to see the teacher that you will one day become, so that you'll know these difficulties are a normal part of any new teacher's experience. Believe it or not, you will overcome these obstacles and succeed.

Let's start our journey by visiting your classroom in the year 2004. Right now, in the year 1981, the year 2004 seems like some futuristic dream, but the world isn't going to be that much different from what you are experiencing now. Even though technology will change the way people communicate and learn, success in the classroom will be based on relationships between students, teachers, and parents. When people step into your classroom of 2004, they see children who enjoy being at school and who are actively engaged in learning. You are teaching fifth grade, and have been for over 10 years. You discovered that the elementary classroom is perfect for your style of teaching, and you love working with fifth grade students. Even after 23 years of teaching, you enjoy each day and look forward to trying out new strategies and getting kids excited about learning. Parents request you for their child's teacher, and you are able to build a strong base of support with those families.

Now let's look at your professional life as an educator in 2004. You were one of the first teachers in your district to earn National Board Certification in 1998, and you have served as a mentor to other teachers attempting to earn this recognition. What about your dream of writing your first book by age 30? You achieved that goal and more, having published six books for teachers by the year 2004! You have provided staff development within your district and across the country in the areas of Cooperative Learning and Literature Circles. Best of all, you won a $25,000 award for excellence in teaching, and you didn't even know that award existed! I'm not going to spoil the surprise by telling you the name of the award or exactly when you received it, but just know that it is going to be one of the most momentous points of your teaching career!

Now let's get back to the present, the year 1981. I wanted you to take a peek into your future to show you that things really are going to get better, but now you could use some real advice. You've got many years ahead of you before you achieve some of your dreams, and I don't want those years to be miserable ones.

First of all, you must recognize that although it's important for you to care for your students, you don't need to be a buddy to them. You must view yourself as an authority figure, because that's what they expect and need. They need firmness and consistency along with your caring attitude. Children will push the limits constantly in order to find out what they can get away with, and if you don't set limits and enforce them consistently, they will become frustrated and angry. You need a classroom management system that will help you let them know when they are going too far. Read *Assertive Discipline* (1992) by Lee Canter for some concrete and practical ideas. You will be tempted to use corporal punishment because the teachers on your grade level use this technique, and you don't want to be considered weak for not paddling your students. Don't do it! You will regret those actions later, because spanking children does not solve the basic problems that cause them to be the way they are. A caring attitude and a firm, consistent discipline policy are much more effective than corporal punishment.

Next, it's important to associate with other educators who demonstrate a caring, positive attitude toward students and who love the profession. Don't hang around with teachers who spew their negativity on anyone who will listen. Don't be drawn into saying negative things about your students or other teachers; those kinds of comments have a way of coming back to haunt you. Find people who feel the way you do, and spend time sharing ideas with them. In the future, you will have a unique way of sharing with other teachers through something called the Internet, a computer-based communication system. Be one of those educators on the cutting edge of technology both in the classroom and in your personal life. The Internet will provide you with a support system that is beyond your imagination, but until then you will have to find people within your school and school system who can support you as a new teacher. They are there; just seek them out.

Finally, focus on taking baby steps this year in your journey as a teacher. The first year is truly the most difficult because you have made many mistakes, and it's difficult to undo them with your current students. Next year you'll have a brand-new class, and your year will be 100% better. Each year will continue to get easier and easier, and before long you will be eager to go to school each day instead of dreading it. As you improve your classroom management, you will be able to relax the structure of your classroom a bit and allow more freedom and interaction between students. This type of classroom is what you dreamed of in college, but it can't happen until you solve the management issues that are causing your difficulties. Don't be afraid to ask your principal for help because he believes in you and will support you.

In the future, you'll discover that the wonderful thing about being a teacher is the way you continue to learn and grow along with your students. No matter how many years you're in the classroom, you can always reflect on what you are doing and find a better way. It's the most creative, challenging, and rewarding profession I know, and being a teacher will be a source of joy in your life. Instead of dreading each day, learn from your mistakes and move on. Believe in yourself and have faith in the teacher you will one day become!

Sincerely,
Laura Candler (Older and Wiser)
September 27, 2004

References _____

Canter, L., & Canter, M. (1992). *Assertive discipline: Positive behavior management for today's classroom*. Seal Beach, CA: Lee Canter & Associates.

This letter writer set the stage for receiving the letter she wrote to her younger self.

It finally happened—a chance to do what I had always dreamed! The phone call that forever changed my life and the lives of many young children. "Ms. Reece, we would like to offer you a position as our Grammar and Writing teacher for Grades 4–8," said my soon-to-be principal and now mentor. As I fell to my knees, an overflowing rush of joy, relief, exhilaration, and pure unequivocal gratitude overcame me at an instant. I had always known that I wanted to be a teacher, but with no classroom experience it was difficult finding a position. So, when she said those unforgettable words to me, my emotional rollercoaster was inescapable. However, although I was filled with an immeasurable feeling of excitement for my newly acquired teaching position, as the school year drew near, I began to experience a multitude of thoughts about whether or not I was really even qualified to do the job for which I had been called. But, nonetheless, my first year of teaching began. Now, seven years later, I am still in the classroom teaching. But, in an ideal world, if my younger self had the chance to walk into her classroom on her first day of teaching again, I hope she would find this letter on her desk . . .

Dear Ms. Reece,

Congratulations on this professional milestone! I am aware you have been awaiting this opportunity for years now, and I am thrilled about your future as a teacher. As you embark on this professional journey, I would like to offer some words of advice and encouragement. It is my hope that my words not only help you become the most effective teacher possible, but that you are able to grow as a young woman as well. Teaching can have many rewards, but the challenges that come with the job are innumerable. With that in mind, my first charge to you is to always ask questions.

In the profession of teaching, change is inevitable. Therefore, do not be fearful of asking your administrators and even fellow colleagues for assistance with understanding new policies and procedures as it relates to various matters in your school. As the old saying goes, "there is no such thing as a dumb question." Well, you will find later that this may not always apply to your students, but for you, ask even if you think you are sure of the answer. The feeling of anxiety and stress over questions to which you do not have the answers is one you want to avoid if at all possible. So, when in doubt, ask.

Now, an important word in the field of teaching is the "f" word. You are probably wondering what the "f" word is exactly and how it will help you as a teacher. Flexibility is the "f" word. Calendars change, students are moved from one class to another, new students enroll, testing schedules change, and the list is infinite. You may have the perfect lesson planned, for the perfect day, and to your unpleasant surprise, a pep rally or an assembly has been scheduled. Flexibility is crucial when handling the ever-increasing spontaneity of a school's day-to-day activities. It is important to be open-minded to changes, as everything will get finished, eventually. You will be able to teach that "perfect lesson," but do not become discouraged if it does not happen on the "perfect day." Know that some changes are unavoidable, and at times, supersede other plans you may have for your students. This may be difficult to understand now, but a flexible teacher is an effective teacher. The ability to make changes or adjust as needed allows for invaluable opportunities to reevaluate lessons, activities, and other plans.

Flexibility not only applies to day-to-day schedule and activities, but to grading papers as well. Grading can be an overwhelming task for any teacher, let alone a first-year teacher. But, again, be flexible. Every assignment does not have to be graded immediately. Manage your time accordingly and prioritize assignments. Also, know that each individual assignment does not require a numerical grade. This may seem like an unorthodox strategy and even unpopular, but you must think of grading in terms of assessments. If a student has completed an assignment and demonstrated their knowledge of a skill successfully, they simply need acknowledgement of this, which does not necessarily have to be numerical. Utilize stamps, stickers, and other quick tools to acknowledge students' work, which will increase grading efficiency tremendously.

Efficiency is important when grading, but, avoid, if at all possible, exchanging the peace and sanctity of your home for increased grading efficiency. Taking papers home to grade is a common error made by many first-year teachers and even experienced teachers. It does not make you a less dedicated teacher if you do not take the work home. As stated before, it will all get finished, eventually. Your home is a place where you should feel relaxed and free from the stresses of the classroom. So, leave those papers where they belong, in the classroom. No doubt they will be where you left them Monday morning, unless the custodial staff is suddenly overcome with an overwhelming desire to grade your students' work.

Although you may be inundated with grading and the many other daily tasks that come with being a teacher, much time will also present itself for you to foster many relationships with your colleagues and students alike. However, as a first-year teacher, it is imperative to understand arguably one of the most challenging relationships that come with the job, which is the parent–teacher relationship. First, when managing the parent–teacher relationship, it is important to understand that, as a teacher, you are dealing with a parent's or guardian's most prized possession, his or her child. Therefore, communications and interactions with parents must have a tone that reflects an understanding of this, in order to accomplish what is in the best interests of the child. Many parents/guardians may approach you in an aggressive, unpleasant, and even downright disrespectful manner. However, remain professional at all times, and learn to keep the student at the forefront.

Parents/guardians must have the feeling that you as the teacher care about their child. As the teacher, you must create this reassurance in parents/guardians through your words and actions. Do not simply make statements; take action and demonstrate your willingness to help the student. You will also want to be sure you are consistent with your contact and communication. Again, this is a relationship, so attentive detail must be paid to how often contact is made, in order to build a strong working relationship between you and the parent, as well as the student. As with almost any relationship, you will experience unpleasant times and experiences. But, stay encouraged and keep your students in mind at all times. Rest assured that your work is for them, the students, not their parents. Foster a positive, professional parent–teacher relationship, but never forget the student.

As important as it is to foster healthy relationships with parents, students, and other members of the school community, it is just as important to have a relationship with an experienced teacher. Specifically, a mentor who can provide advice in all areas of the teaching field. As a first-year teacher, many challenges will arise that may drive you to feeling like throwing in the towel. But, a mentor can provide much needed encouragement and words of wisdom in times, such as the aforementioned, throughout your first year of teaching. For me, Mrs. J. is the mentor of all mentors. I have cried in her office and on her shoulder many days. My countless frustrations have been vented to her free from judgement. She has not only observed me as a teacher in my classroom, but she has helped me become a better teacher by teaching me everything she knows about the craft.

Your mentor should be someone you are comfortable asking for help at any given moment. Someone who is willing to come into your classroom and provide honest, yet constructive feedback to make you a superior teacher. It is vital to your longevity in the field of teaching to have someone willing to invest in you both personally and professionally. In your first year, you want a mentor who will sit in your classroom and not only observe you teach, but jump in and help you when needed. A mentor should make you better by showing you. In all, a mentor–first-year-teacher relationship will help you not only push through your first year professionally, but emotionally and personally as well. My advice, find your Mrs. J.

Now, the final piece of advice I want to leave with you before you embark on this first year of teaching is actually quite simple—have fun. Teaching can be an arduous task; therefore, enjoying each moment in the classroom with your students is essential. You are teaching children, and that is important to keep in mind—they are children. So, listen to a little music every once in a while! Allow your students to see you having a good time in the classroom and enjoying yourself. Break out a dance move every once in a while! Your students may be overly embarrassed of course, but, they have to see that you are human. Tell or make jokes and make fun of yourself when the opportunities present themselves. Laugh at yourself, and let your students laugh at or with you! Also, keep fun knickknacks in your classroom to liven up the environment when needed. I keep mini toy footballs, basketballs, and baseballs in my classroom and often throw them to students who I am selecting to answer questions. I have even had a student ask me to put a miniature basketball hoop in my classroom, which truthfully is not such a bad idea. You can even keep hacky sacks in your classroom, as children also love these types of objects. In all, it is acceptable to enjoy yourself and enjoy your students. After all, you all are going to be spending an abundance of time with one another over the next few months, so you might as well have some fun while you're stuck with each other!

In sum, I hope this first year of teaching is memorable and life-changing. Teaching is a noble profession that often receives insufficient recognition. But, you are boldly taking on one of the most difficult tasks, which is shaping the young minds of tomorrow. The children who are going to walk into your classroom are the future of this great nation, and you are where their future begins. Stay encouraged, remain positive, and never stop smiling! For me, teaching was first just a dream, and now it is a reality. I have found this quotation to be true: "For only those who dare to dream can make their dreams come true."—Author unknown.

Much success on your first year,
Your future and wiser self,
Domonique Reece

Dear Beginning Teacher James,

Wow!! How time has flown since I started my career as a teacher! I have been a teacher, an assistant principal, and a principal. Now I am an associate professor at an extraordinary university in North Carolina. All of the things that your professors teach you in college are important; however, when you land your first teaching job, you learn a lot of things from personal experience and authentic interactions within the school building.

I can remember my first job as a teacher. I was worried that I wouldn't be able to control the students and that when my principal came in to observe me that I would just freeze. But you know what? That didn't happen at all. I was blessed with great mentors and colleagues who helped me as a newbie to learn the ropes and encouraged me to try out some of my interesting and nontraditional instructional strategies. Most of them actually worked, too! There are a few things that I think are important for every new teacher to know. With some of the items, I always had them at the forefront of my mind, and with others, throughout the passing years, I've worked to keep thinking about them regularly. Some big-ticket items for me, and YOU:

- Relationships, relationships, relationships—they matter more than any other indicator.
- Teach procedures and routines at the beginning of the year and throughout the year.
- Maintain great classroom management, because without it, not much else matters.
- Plan and execute engaging lessons (easier said than done).
- Never stop learning. This can fall off of a full teacher's "plate" when things get busy, but lifelong learning is one of the strongest investments we can make!

First, let's talk about meaningful, purposeful relationships. Positive relationships with students will cause them to work harder for you, therefore, impacting their academic achievement, and it will also cause your students to be better behaved, helping you to strengthen your classroom management skills. Building relationships is one of the most important things you can do as a teacher, principal, or professor. You need to get to know your students well and let them know that you care about them. Young James, you were great at building relationships, and you continue to build them even today. Use your knowledge of your students to plan your lessons and help to get them engaged in the learning. You trained yourself well at remembering the following: Even when you are just starting out, it is important to say "YES" when you can, to students. Don't say "NO," just because you can. Things improve when you say "YES." Whenever you can say "YES" in an ongoing manner, it makes the "NO" easier to handle when it comes along. You also need to build relationships with your students' parents. They know their children better than anyone, and they can be your greatest supporters (these relationships will help you when disciplinary issues roll around, too).

You also need to build relationships with the school staff, especially the school secretary and the custodian. I must have heard that a hundred times from veteran teachers when I was entering the classroom that first year. These individuals are vital to your role as a successful, life-changing teacher. The school secretary helps you keep supplies in your classroom, and the custodian keeps your room clean (your work environment was always clean and invitational). It is also vital to have beneficial relationships with your team of teachers at your specific grade level. You will be together every single day, and being a team player is vital to your success. The administrative staff is extremely important as well. You need to know exactly what they expect and be attentive in meetings and professional development sessions. Don't attend meetings and then text, grade papers, or talk. School principals notice these things, and actions like this don't shine a flattering light on new teachers. The administrators are looking for teacher leaders, and building those relationships can put you on their radar.

As you climb the ladder, the need to build relationships does not go away. You not only need to build relationships with students, parents, and staff, but you also have to build solid relationships with your school's stakeholders and community. These relationships can go a long way to building bridges for donations and community support for your school. I can remember the payoff being huge when I asked local churches, banks, realtors, and grocery stores for all kinds of donations ranging from food to school supplies. I had to remind myself, "You have not, because you ask not." There was a constant flow of donated items into my classroom; index cards, paper, composition books, snacks, construction paper, and bottled water. The list really did go on and on. It's hard to teach without quality "stuff," so pour yourself into building relationships, and then work them to your advantage.

As we transition to classroom management, this was one area that really came quite naturally to me. Teaching routines and procedures are highly important parts of your classroom operations. Again, easy to say, but harder to do. You have to be aware of what you are saying, what you are doing, and if you are getting the desired results from students. Be reflective and, again, purposeful with your processes and procedures.

Students need to know what you expect, and you need to be consistent with those expectations. If you want students to enter your classroom quietly and quickly get into their seats, you must practice this procedure until it becomes a natural routine. You must decide ahead of time what you want your classroom to look like, and then put those procedures into practice. One way to decide what you want your classroom to look and feel like is to observe effective teachers or watch videos of truly champion teachers. You need to make each procedure your own, and then teach your students your expectations. Procedures should be explicitly taught during the first 10 days of school and then brought back out during the year when the need arises. In the end, say what you mean, and mean what you say.

Classroom management is a MUST in your classroom if you want to be an effective teacher, and it goes hand-in-hand with the procedural "stuff" mentioned above. Students cannot learn in chaos. Order and procedures with consistent consequences and celebrations need to be in place in your classroom. It is fine to have your students help make the rules (at times), but just be sure that the rules that you want for your classroom are among the ones you agree on. Three to five rules are plenty. Settle for nothing less than 100% of what you want when it comes to classroom management.

Once the rules are chosen, then teach those rules and what your expectations are. You can also discuss the consequences for breaking those rules (always have an effective consequence ready, just in case, so you are never caught off guard). Make sure when your students leave your classroom to travel to another area of the school, such as the cafeteria, the Media Center, the computer lab, or other areas, that they walk in a straight line with no talking.

Help your students understand the need for the straight line and no talking. If you make it meaningful, they will most likely comply. It is more than a straight line. It is about how we carry ourselves, what others see in us, and how we set ourselves apart.

Keep in mind now, becoming an effective teacher does not happen overnight, and it takes a great deal of hard work. In order to be effective, you must plan lessons that align with your state standards and are engaging for your students. Your lessons must meet the needs of every student in your classroom. This means that you will need to differentiate your lessons to meet the skill levels of each student in your classroom. There are many engaging strategies that can be utilized to motivate and inspire your students. Make sure you allow your students to work in small groups and collaborate. This collaboration will help them be ready for the real world.

Using repetition is very important in helping your students learn new content. You also need to attempt to use your students' learning styles to meet their needs. Utilize graphic organizers, diagrams, and other stimuli to engage your visual learners. Use turn-and-talks and discussion groups, or have students record their notes and listen to them to engage those auditory learners. Finally, use hands-on experiments, tactile activities, and real-life examples to help your kinesthetic learners. Do not be satisfied with the status quo. Go above and beyond to engage every learner in your classroom. **They deserve your very best, every day**!

Finally, be a lifelong learner. Never quit learning. You are so lucky to have the luxury of the Internet and digital devices in the classroom. I was lucky to have a couple of desktop computers in my classroom in my early days. As a teacher learner, we need to evolve with the landscape around us. Get engaged with all required professional development and search out other professional development that interests you. Get involved in Professional Learning Communities (you know, those PLCs) at your school and district level and learn as much as you can. Share your learning with others. Share your supplies with others. Become a true learning community, and do what is best for kids.

My mission statement is a simple one: *Love Kids, Support Teachers, Involve Parents, and Pass It On . . .*

All of the ideas that I have shared with you, my younger self, adhere to this mission statement. *Love Kids*—Build those relationships, maintain orderly and safe classrooms, and engage them in well-planned lessons. When you love kids, you do anything that you can for them. You feed them, teach them well, offer a coat when they are cold, and you listen to them when they need to talk. *Support Teachers*—Work diligently with colleagues to form a team of support for teachers and say "YES" when you can. Build a learning community, and provide meaningful times for planning, reflection, and the creation of true student-centered action steps. *Involve Parents*—Work to get parents on your side, get their sincere and authentic input, and always keep them in the loop. *Pass It On*—That is what this letter is all about. Passing on the knowledge that was passed on to me by so many of my colleagues, principals, and others along this fabulous journey. Education has been my LIFE, and I want to pass on everything that I have learned to help the teachers and educators of the future.

In closing: Live life daily as you **"Love kids, support teachers, involve parents, and pass it on!"**

With an attitude of gratitude,
Dr. James V. Davis, the older you

Dear Heather,

This is your first day of teaching. You are feeling a combination of excitement and anxiety. Today you are going to walk into your first high school English teaching gig with 12th graders and 10th graders. You have this week's lessons ready, and that's about it. You have 120 new names and personalities to learn, and you hope that you will make a good impression. You are only 24, so you hope the students will see you as an authority figure and not as a pal to invite out to the parties. Oh, and you are lateral entry, which means you are earning your teaching credential while on the job. You have some knowledge of what teaching is about, but you've not gone through student teaching. You don't really even know how to put together a proper teaching lesson. You're thinking, "Why did these people hire me?! Don't they know I'm a fraud?"

Well I'm here to let you know that you are NOT a fraud, and you are worthy. You have something to offer these students, so don't be intimidated by them. You have grit, and that is a key to success in teaching. So, whatever you do, DON'T GIVE UP. It's going to be hard, you are not going to sleep a lot, and you will worry more than is necessary about your students and how you are going to keep up with everything there is to do. But you are going to make it through! Just keep your sense of humor and keep your creativity, and the rest will come.

I want to pass along some advice to you as you start this first year of teaching. First, be flexible. I hate to tell you this, but you are not going to get to work with these particular students beyond the first two weeks of school. There's nothing wrong with you or your teaching; it's just a bit of bad timing. The school isn't going to have enough students to support the number of teachers it hired, so you will have to go. You are going to be transferred to the neighboring middle school. MIDDLE SCHOOL! You are not going to like this, and you are not going to be prepared for the world of silent lunches, girls being taller than boys, and team teaching. But I promise you that it's all going to work out for the best.

You see, this experience, while it will hurt, will end up making you even more resilient. You are going to gain some invaluable skills with behavior management from working with eighth graders. You are going to develop patience for riding out the adolescent wave of hormones that will hit you every day. And you are going to get a 'do-over' with these students so you can correct all the little mistakes you made in the first two weeks with your high-schoolers. It's all going to work out.

Team teaching in middle school is amazing. You will have a fellow young Social Studies teacher on your team who is going to take you under her wing. She's going to give you a crash course in student teaching. My advice for you, teaching newbie, is to reach out to all of your colleagues. Ask them for advice, get them to share lesson ideas and troubleshoot problems you are encountering, and let them offer a friendly ear when you've just had a frustrating day and need to vent. You are now part of a team, and this team looks out for its own. Take advantage and steal as many good ideas as you can. Oh, and don't forget to go observe some teachers during your planning period. It may seem hard to give up that precious planning time, but it's so worth it.

Another piece of advice is to go to workshops. You are new, and you didn't have the benefit of a university teaching degree. So, go to workshops where you can gather great lesson ideas and teaching strategies. Go to practical workshops being offered in your county. You may just find an inspiring lesson that will carry you through that next day or week.

If I could sum up my three major pieces of advice for your first year, it's DON'T GIVE UP, seek help from others, and find ways to stay inspired. The last point is an important one. You are going to be so tired. This job will not end at 5:00 pm. Even when you go home, you will think about your students, even dream about them! You will find yourself using your "teacher voice" to an unappreciative family member one day. It's hard to turn off the teacher. All of this can be exhausting, and it's a marathon, not a sprint. So, find things to inspire you. Maybe it's a creative lesson idea, like a debate or an artistic project using Shakespearean sonnets. Try to find something that will keep your excitement up for your classes. Worksheets and lectures may be "easy" ways to teach, but they hardly inspire. If you are inspired, your students will also be inspired. Joy and enthusiasm are contagious, so find ways to stay fresh.

Outside of teaching, I'd like to offer you a few practical suggestions for helping you through that initial year. First, invest in a good massage from time to time. It's so worth it. Also, it will be hard to eat well because you are so busy. Try not to eat out of the snack machine all day. Take time to pack some healthy snacks to nibble on at school. That freshman 15 (adding on those dreaded extra pounds) happens again the first year of teaching! Have a social life, and go out with friends. Go dancing. It's important that you have an outlet and life outside of school. Go to the gym. This will be hard during your first year. The only time you can make it work will be BEFORE school. You are NOT a morning person, so this will be a challenge. And my final piece of advice is to go to bed early. Sleep is key to survival your first year. Friday nights are for a good dinner out and an early bedtime. There's no shame in that!

I hope this letter is an encouragement to you on this first day of school. You may have some tough times this year, but you will use everything you learned to help other new teachers. So, it's all going to come together, even though you may not understand this at the time.

Good luck this year, and know that your older self has no regrets for your choices. So, teach BIG and don't be afraid to take chances and make mistakes. You are going to be great!

Your older, more experienced self,
Heather Higgins Lynn

Greetings and Salutations!

As a new teacher, I found the world of education full of exciting possibilities. Like so many beginning teachers, I entered the field full of hope in my ability to make a difference and to spend time in a subject I love so much—*social studies*. Yet, the realities of the daily grind and actual students can prove to be challenging, even daunting. The reality check, as it were, often comes in the most unexpected ways and can leave a new teacher feeling drained and full of doubt. As I am sure you can relate, I found myself both overwhelmed and energized with the prospects of beginning a career in education.

In this letter, I wish to share with you—my first-year-teacher self—some **essential ideas** I wish I had known from the start and things I learned along the way that I have found invaluable. As I reflect, I hope you see how my—OUR—experiences have made ME/US better educators and a better human being in the world. *Remember* (future self) . . . **growth is essential to wisdom**.

When I first wanted to get into teaching, I remember one of my professors stating, "you have to love kids" to be a good teacher. When I first heard this declaration, I did not really understand. It seemed I still had some learning to do.

I always knew I wanted to be a teacher. I clearly remember playing school as a young child and loving the idea of being a part of this wonderful world of education. It spoke to my soul. Somewhere along the way, however, as I got older I questioned that calling. As a result, I did not enter the classroom until I was older. Sometimes I wish I had gotten into education sooner, but . . . *Remember* (future self) . . . **everything happens for a reason**.

Like so many other young adults with ambitions to teach high school, I loved my content. I had great imaginings of being this dynamic lecturer who would inspire a love of history in my students. I could not have been more wrong. While I had always loved history, the classes I did enjoy the most were when the teacher brought the story to life. I felt like I was part of something bigger than myself and that I was gaining access to the secrets of the past. I also felt like I understood the world of today better by knowing the events of the past. Even when things did not always make sense or the teacher was boring, I still took joy in the learning. When I entered the classroom, I wanted to impart my knowledge to my students and share with them all the exciting events of the past and help them to understand how the world we now know came to be. I failed to understand, however, *two very important things*. I failed to **appreciate the ways in which I was so very different from my students** *and* I failed to **understand that teaching is about so much more than knowing and sharing content knowledge**.

In my first days in the classroom, I quickly learned that the way in which I experienced school was not the same as the way in which many of my students experienced school. I was a "good kid" who benefitted from the meritocracy of schooling (Lindsay Toth & Cinnamon-Morrison, 2011). Initially, I could not understand why my students resisted their "education." Soon, I began to realize that *my idea*s of education were really more in line with schooling—and there is a huge difference between schooling and getting an education. For my students, school was an oppressive place that privileged silent obedience and seemed to have no interest in them as individuals; they had no interest in complying with rules they viewed as being *imposed* on them.

Sometimes it is difficult to understand why a teenager might resist the wisdom of adults or why they might fail to understand the importance of their education. We, as teachers, enter the profession because we believe in our education system and in the importance of an education. It can seem almost inconceivable that someone—*anyone*—would not want to improve themselves or value their education. What we as teachers fail to realize are the ways in which schools and schooling can be harmful to some children, especially children of color. *Remember* (future self) . . . **not everyone sees the world in the same way**.

Regardless of the student, the old adage, "*People don't care how much you know until they know how much you care*," rings especially true for adolescents. Noddings (1988) argues for an ethic of caring "that is directly concerned with the relations in which we all must live" where the growth of the student is a central concern to the teacher (p. 219). She asks us to the consider relationships that we as teachers have with our students as a key element in providing a positive learning environment. She rightfully claims that the schooling experience goes well beyond the teaching of academic skills; it includes moral and citizenship education. As I tried—and failed many times—to understand my students, my role in the classroom, and my own ideas about education and school, I came to understand that caring about students mattered more than anyone ever says, or perhaps realizes. I wish I had known about Noddings' ethic of care early on. She has helped me to fully embrace the idea that teachers ought to show concern for their students as people, work to help prepare them to be contributing members of society, and be interested in them as individuals. *Remember* (future self) . . . **you have to care about your students**.

When I started taking an interest in my students and their lives, they began to take an interest in me *AND* in their learning. I came to understand that my role as their teacher went beyond the narrow scope of teaching content and skills, just as Noddings (1988) says. I also came to realize that, as the adult or authority in the classroom, I was also reinforcing certain societal values, training my students how to act and interact both with and as adults in a broadly social way, and showing them how to act as citizens in more formal spaces. By better understanding who they were as people, I found myself better able to teach and engage them in actually learning. At one point, I felt like an untrained counselor, but really I was just *engaging my students as human beings* and actually *caring about who they were* and what their lives were like beyond my classroom. When I practiced an ethic of caring, my students came to care about me too. Over time, we created a classroom environment where they trusted my *intentions*. They then trusted *me*. Once I had earned their trust, they wanted to learn from me. **Bottom line**: *You have to show you care*. Show that you love kids (that professor was right). You won't make it in this career if you don't.

As I came to realize that the world of school that I knew is not the reality for everyone, I began to also understand the ways in which I was actually harming some of my student's educational experiences and the ways in which I was both reinforcing and using what Delpit (2006) calls the *"culture of power"* to alienate and silence my students. Those underlying "codes of conduct" and "expectations of behavior" are actually a *hidden curriculum* in schools that serve as socializing force for (or against) students. Students are taught to conform to certain behavioral standards, expectations, and values that "shape and influence practically every aspect of the student's educational experience" (Giroux & Penna, 1979).

While many components of a *hidden curriculum* may operate as a way to impart normative standards of acceptable behavior and a way to promote a seemingly shared value system that exists in larger society, this *hidden curriculum* can also serve as a site of oppression. For example, in most school settings, students are expected to raise their hand and wait for permission to speak. I had always accepted this act as "the way" to have my voice heard in class; it even seemed like a reasonable rule—*to me*. In fact, this idea of *waiting my turn* to speak was often reinforced at home. I waited, got my turn, and I was always heard. I did not know that—for other students—particularly some students of color—this act of *waiting your turn* actually served as a way to silence voices. In some households, one has to just *jump in* and start talking in order to be heard. It begs the question—*whose values are actually being taught in this hidden curriculum? Remember* (future self) . . . **we are teaching values, and they show up in everything we do.**

These disconnects between *expectations at home* versus *expectations in school* can be highly problematic, especially for students whose ethnic or cultural identity are not that of the dominant social group. While I sensed this tension in my own classroom, I could not quite put my finger on what was really happening until I read Lisa Delpit's *Other People's Children*. Her descriptions of the ways in which people from different ethnic and cultural backgrounds understand school differently than my own experiences helped me make sense of the disconnect I was feeling with my students. I wish I had come across her message much earlier upon entering the classroom.

I also quickly realized that "knowing" a subject and *knowing how to teach* it are not the same thing. Just because I knew a lot about history and loved the subject did not mean that I knew anything about pedagogy, that is, how to teach. All too often, adults enter the teaching profession without understanding the fundamental differences between teaching and learning, or even what really goes into good teaching. Sure, we all may have had the good fortune of benefitting from a truly good teacher, but too few of us as a society really know what goes into teaching. To this end, *pedagogy and professionalism are essential. Remember* (future self) . . . **you don't know as much as you think you do**.

Imagine for a moment that you walk into a doctor's office and the person before you says this: "I have read lots of anatomy books, and I have been going to doctors for years. So I know how to practice medicine." I do not imagine anyone would be too keen on allowing that so-called doctor to treat and diagnose oneself, let alone anyone else. Yet, this scenario plays itself out in the world of teaching far too often. Many outside the world of education fail to appreciate that teaching is a profession and requires practice, skill, and training. Content knowledge is only one aspect of what is needed. Pedagogical and professional knowledge are the other two key aspects that make a teacher *good*. Learn good pedagogy. It will take care of most discipline problems in the classroom. *Remember* (future self) . . . **pedagogy matters**.

Teaching is an art. This is the most important thing that I learned along the way. There is an element of performance in everything we do as teachers. As I began to ponder how to reach my students effectively, I came to realize that if I let go of my own ego—*and my fears*—I could let my passion for my content shine through. I learned this lesson through learning about pedagogy.

When I encountered other educators who demonstrated a profound passion for their work and genuine interest in their students, I also noticed that these same educators truly enjoyed being in the classroom every day. Even more importantly, they made learning fun! To do this, they were masters at asking questions and keeping students engaged. They were not afraid to make funny faces, role play, sing off key, or use gestures to act out some material. This is not to say that learning was a show, but rather that they used a lot of tools in their pedagogical toolboxes to make the learning relatable and understandable to the students.

We are now firmly rooted in the world of the 21st century. In many ways, it is a vastly different world than that of the 20th century. I think it is important to *remember* that, too. Today's young children are living in and experiencing a different world—*a new reality*—than that of the 20th century. We "adults" may reminisce about the "good ole days," but the truth is, such fantasies are the purview of elders, a re-remembering of their past as idyllic. Every generation, however, has its own struggles and has to (re-)define its own reality. Just as we did when we were young. In this respect, the best advice I can think to give to you, my future self, is: **Never grow old. Stay fresh. Grow**. Recognize that your students' experiences are not yours—and your students, our future, have something to say about that. Always be the best you that you can be, and, above all, *REMEMBER THESE THREE THINGS*:

Love your students.

Be artful in your teaching.

Listen.

Cheers!

Serina A. Cinnamon

References

Delpit, Lisa D. (2006). *Other people's children: Cultural conflict in the classroom.* New York: The New Press.

Giroux, H. A., & Penna, A. N. (1979). Social education in the classroom: The dynamics of the hidden curriculum. *Theory & Research in Social Education, 7*(1), 21–42

Lindsay Toth, S., & Cinnamon Morrison, S. (2011). The elephant in the room: a conundrum in democratic teaching and learning. *Scholar-Practitioner Quarterly, 5*(4), 347–359.

Noddings, N. (1988). An ethic of caring and its implications for instructional arrangements. *American Journal of Education, 96*(2), 215–230.

Dear Disorganized, Decisive, Delirious, Diplomatic, Doubtful Donna,

I am fond of the old saying, "If you could start over with the knowledge that you have now, what would be different?" I can state that there are things that I would change and things that I would keep the same. In my career as an educator, I have grown through the years. I do not want to erase all the gained knowledge, but I would like to have a chance to do some things differently.

"Plan, plan, plan," are words that need to be branded into a teacher's brain. It is essential for new teachers to have plans for each day that attempt to meet the needs of students. Plan with the curriculum, and keep in mind a purpose for what students should know. I thought that I had this under control until one day I realized while doing a literature selection that students did not have a clue about what I expected them to gain from the story. When one of the students asked what they were supposed to understand about the story, I realized that what was as clear to me as a crystal glass was just muddy water to the students. I realized that many of the lessons that I had done were not clear to students; without a purpose, students are in the dark.

Being a lifelong learner is a key to improvement. As an educator, I find I am constantly learning about effective instructional practices that help students to learn. As a teacher, you will have to develop a professional library, filled with books that have dog-eared pages, to assist you with practices that are research-based and improve instruction. Find time to read those professional magazines, even if it is while you are waiting for the copier to spit out the pages of torture for your students.

Other words to live by are, "Expect the unexpected." The "last minute" is an enemy of new teachers, but it is the motto that they live by. That last minute is when the copier will break down, or the parent will decide to show up for a conference, or the principal decides that you need to attend this meeting to learn new strategies. On the other hand, the last minute is when some teachers develop the best lesson plan, because they have changed it after it crashed and burned with the first block's class.

Humor is the way to survive. Without humor, the world would stop spinning. I have learned that there are times that I need to laugh at myself instead of crying. If I can laugh, I know it will get better. Laughter is good for the brain. It helps to keep things from getting too serious.

Another key point is to realize that teaching is like a road. There are bumpy spots, and twist and turns, but then there are times when it will be smooth navigating. Do not expect things to always go well; if it did there would be no challenge, and your life would be boring. You may have to switch lanes from time to time, but stay true to the road, and you will get to your destination in the end, which is the achievement of all students.

Take this knowledge that I donate to you, and get ready for the ride of your life!

Sincerely,
Donna Gephart

Dear Mychael,

Your first year teaching was quite an experience, to say the least! You had just graduated college and were looking forward to what the future would hold for you and your son. The optimism level was off the charts. Then one day you received a call, a call that would change your life forever. Do you remember that? I know, I know, how could you forget? You were hired as a high school biology teacher. The fact that the school was your rival high school didn't mean anything because ... WE GOT A JOB! WE GOT A JOB!"

A few weeks before the start date, you got to intern under a science teacher there. It was awesome! You went home and began to lesson plan before you even knew what that meant. Remember how you would force friends and family to listen to you deliver your future lessons. They were so annoyed with you, but oh well. You already had begun a very essential part of good teaching, being reflective. Right before you were supposed to start, you got a phone call that you would be teaching physical science and NOT biology. Physical science?

Physical Science!?! E-w-w-w . . . chemistry, physics, and math. Every course you dreaded in college. Not even close to what you had been preparing for. All that practicing for nothing, but because you're such a trooper, you started from square one, not knowing much of the subject area, and you did so without complaining. At least not a lot of complaining . . . out loud. You began to experience another part of teaching that still holds true, being fluid. At the end of the semester, you administered the final exam. It wasn't until October of the following school year that you found out your students not only met growth but exceeded it as well. You hit the blue! You go girl! You did a great job, and I am so very proud of you, but there were some—well a LOT—of teachable moments during that semester that I have since reflected on.

One thing that I stress now is my rapport with my students and colleagues. Because you are naturally a people person, that was something you never struggled with. Do you remember Ben? Well, he came to see me . . . you . . . us . . . a few weeks ago. He has adjusted very well to life in college. He even went into the science field. Can you believe that? Anyway, for every student you positively impacted, a few things stick out to me now. In your effort to motivate the kids to be the best versions of themselves, you became impatient with students who didn't. It wasn't your place to make struggling students feel bad for your perceived idea that they were not trying. There were some students who were legitimately trying and just didn't understand what you were teaching. To make them feel even more inadequate in front of their peers was irresponsible and very immature of you. You went from trying to motivate them to almost shaming them. That wasn't, and will never, be okay. You should have always made sure your classroom was a safe and inviting place for all of your students, not just the ones you felt were trying their best. You should have also kept in mind that a lot of the students enrolled at this high school have poor home lives, with parents who are almost nonexistent. Dealing with what they do at home and then still making it to school takes a lot for them. A smile and a positive remark goes a long way and changes the atmosphere in the classroom. It was also very arrogant of you to assume the reason they weren't doing well was only because they were not trying. Let me to tell you something, Mychael. Some of those lesson plans—if we can call them that—along with your lessons, were rushed, last minute, and confusing. I think one of the reasons I have such good ones now is because you've already showed me what not to do. I believe that lesson plans should be a valuable part of any teacher's daily instructions. You lost sight of being reflective, and I will make sure to not repeat your mistake.

I mentioned parents earlier in a negative manner, but don't get it confused; parents are an integral part of the classroom and should be treated as such. You definitely underutilized them, as do most teachers. Some of the behavioral issues you had, I'm not experiencing now because students know that I have a relationship with their parents and won't hesitate to call mom or dad. Had you done this, it would have saved you money on wine and Tylenol. When behavior issues arose, the way you dealt with it was pretty bad. I wish I could've saved you from some of the confrontations you had with your students. You allowed them to get under your skin way too easily, and you let them know it. Honestly, you looked silly at times arguing with teenagers. Now, I still don't have all the answers to classroom management just yet. Lord knows, I wish I did, but your first year teaching was the last time I argued with a student. The second you do that, you have lost all control of your classroom.

Now don't get upset with me. I know you may be, but I wanted to tell you that you are amazing. You obviously love what you do, and it shows. Not to mention you did all of this with a toddler at home! Your students know it, and that's why they work hard for you. Thank you for teaching me what worked and what absolutely didn't work. I love you and will always reflect on what you've taught me to make me a well-rounded teacher.

Much love,
Your future self
(Mychael Strickland)

Dear Valjeaner,

As I reflect over the years on my educational career, I would like to think that I have gained some wisdom and insights traveling on this educational journey, a journey of a lifetime. There are a vast number of things that I would do differently, if I had an opportunity to start over again, or if I knew then what I know now. I am of the belief that if one wants to have different results, then one must do things differently.

I will begin my letter to you, my former, novice-teacher self, with this quote, *Only the Brave Should Teach*:

"Only the brave should teach. Only those who love the young should teach. Teaching is a vocation. It is as sacred as priesthood; as innate a desire, as inescapable as the genius which compels a great artist. If he has not the concern for humanity, the love of living creatures, the vision of the priest and the artist, he must not teach."—Pearl S. Buck

In my role now as a university professor, there are thought-provoking questions that I pose to novice teachers. "Does it take courage to teach? Do you need to be brave to teach?" My answer is, "Yes, indeed, it does take courage to teach, and yes, one needs to be brave to teach." I would also pose the question, "Is teaching an art or is teaching a science?" As I have grown professionally over the years, my answers have changed. I believe that teaching is an art as well as a science.

Throughout my educational journey, I have learned to be a reflective practitioner. If I were to begin my trip again, I would ask more questions. I implore you to reflect on your teaching practices at the end of each day. Ask yourself, "What worked well in class today? What did not work well in class today? What could I have done differently to make the lesson more effective? How can I modify my lesson tomorrow to make it better?" As I continued on this journey, I have discovered that what worked in the past does not necessarily work with today's students. I was advised by my clinical teachers, "Do not smile until Christmas." This was before there was a "Block" schedule or an "A" or "B" schedule. Since teaching is a part of who I am, and teaching is a part of my character, it would be virtually impossible for me not to smile from August to December. That is not who I am. I advise you to be true to who you are. What works for your colleague down the hall may not necessarily work for you.

It is OK to let your students know that you are human, that you can actually smile, you can actually laugh. Having a sense of humor in the classroom is a must for today's students. I would encourage you to laugh at yourself in class if you make a mistake. A caveat to laughing is to laugh with your students, not at your students, if they make a mistake or cannot answer your questions. Do not use sarcasm or embarrass your students. Admit that you do not have an answer for every question that your students may ask you. It is permissible to say, "I do not know; however, I will research that." Your students will respect you more if you admit that you do not know rather than to pretend to know.

I have discovered throughout my journey that as a young, novice teacher, you do not have to be your students' friend or buddy; they do not have to like you. If your students like you, that is "icing on the cake." However, it is much more to your advantage if they respect you. Your students will respect you more if they know that you respect them as individuals. I am reminded of one of my favorite poets, Maya Angelou, and one of her famous quotes, "I've learned that people will forget what you said, people will forget what you did, but people will never forget how you made them feel." I would go further to say that your students will never forget how you made them feel as an individual person. Your students do not care what you know until they know that you care about them as individuals. They need to know how you will treat them in your classroom. I often pose the question to my university students, "Do you treat all students the same?" They will often answer "yes" without fully processing the question. I once believed that the answer was "yes" and that you should treat all students the same. However, as I have continued on my educational journey, I have determined that the answer is "no," you do not treat all students the same because all students do not have the same needs. As an educator, you will discover that as long as you treat your students equitably, free from bias, prejudice, and discrimination, you are treating them fairly as individuals.

Over the years, I have held on to the concept of the *three R's*: *Rigor*, *Relationships*, and *Relevance*. Your pedagogical approach should be rigorous enough to challenge your students to think critically. You should develop a healthy relationship with your students in that you are approachable enough that they will feel comfortable in discussing an issue with you that may or may not pertain to your academic content. Your delivery should be relevant enough to your students as to make it applicable to their everyday lives where they will be able to make a connection. As you strategically develop your lesson plans, start with the end in mind. What do you want your students to know after the completion of your delivery?

I would encourage you to collaborate with colleagues. Teaching in isolation, as I did when I began this journey, was frightening. I sometimes felt that I was in a maze wandering on my own, trying to figure out what was working and what was not working. I would sometimes feel ashamed if I found myself struggling with a concept or lesson that needed improvement. I surmised over time that the "shame" was to struggle alone. You will learn to work in teams and connect with a mentor. You are not in this alone; a sharing of ideas is a part of the teaching profession. Learning to confer with your colleagues is priceless, as everyone brings something of value to the table, and the support that you receive from a colleague can make a monumental difference in your professional journey. You will learn that the camaraderie that you develop with colleagues is an invaluable resource.

As a change agent and a facilitator of learning, you never stop learning. Develop instructional strategies and techniques through professional development. I encourage you to subscribe to professional scholarly journals, as you will be introduced to a wealth of methodologies that are research-based and that can be utilized in your classroom to enhance and strengthen your professional growth. You should be growing along with your students. I have come to realize that students today are much smarter than my students were when I initially started on this journey. Perhaps it is because of the age of technology, as students are only a click away from researching answers that once took days to find. To sharpen your skills, you must always strive for self-improvement.

As a facilitator of learning, I have come to the realization that it is extremely important to have "balance" in one's life. Find time to meet with colleagues and friends outside of the classroom. Nurture your mental and physical well-being to avoid "teacher burnout." Take care of yourself physically, mentally, and spiritually, as it will enable you to be a more effective teacher. You will need a strong support group with family, friends, and colleagues when this journey presents tremendous challenges, and you may feel as though you want to give up. They will give you the strength to persevere.

There are several characteristics that personify good teaching. I chose a few that I have found to be essential as I embarked on this new exhilarating, exciting, and sometimes challenging and frightening journey, which, at the same time, I found to be rewarding, fulfilling, and the highlight of my life. These characteristics that will help you to make a difference in a child's life are:

- Be prepared;
- Always maintain a positive attitude;
- Teach to all of your students, not just a few;
- Maintain a sense of humor;
- Treat your students equitably;
- Show empathy and a sense of compassion;
- Admit that you are human capable of making mistakes;
- Make each challenge an opportunity to grow.

Sincerely,
Valjeaner Brewington Ford

References _____

Pearl S. Buck. (n.d.). "Only the Brave Should Teach" Retrieved April 17, 2017, from www.lewrockwell.com/2003/05/linda-schrock-taylor/only-the-brave-should-teach

Maya Angelou. (n.d.). BrainyQuote.com. Retrieved April 17, 2017, from https://www.brainyquote.com/quotes/quotes/m/mayaangelo392897.html

Dear Novice Teacher Glenda,

I am writing to you today to share the wisdom I have gained from the experiences I have had over many years in this wonderful profession. I hope that you will find this advice helpful to you as you embark on the exciting career you have chosen. Take heed, novice teacher!

As I reflect on the beliefs that started my educational journey, it is clear that they have evolved over time into an eclectic approach that focuses on student achievement. A learning environment that supports diversity, structure, real-life curriculum, and ongoing assessment is critical to the success of each individual student.

Education should not be the same for everyone in a classroom. To be a responsible teacher means looking at the diverse needs of each student. All students have special learning needs that include learning disabilities, giftedness, culture, as well as socio-economic concerns. The most important thing to remember is that students come in many different packages, and it is the responsibility of the teacher to discover their learning needs.

One way to meet the learning needs of students is to provide an environment that encourages participation and provides a challenge. A flexible classroom that allows students to learn in a whole group, independently, and with partners will motivate students. Teachers need to create a climate that encourages cooperation and celebrates the success of all students.

A structured classroom that uses both rewards and discipline will motivate and encourage students to achieve. By setting certain ground rules within the classroom, a teacher is not only earning respect, but also giving respect. The students will know what to expect and will more than likely strive to meet the teacher's expectations. Rewards encourage students to not only do their work, but to do the right thing even when no one is watching. Discipline provides the guidelines needed for students to succeed.

A curriculum that is research-based and combined with real-life experiences will meet the academic, social, and moral needs of students. It is imperative that all subject areas are covered and applied to everyday life. This approach to teaching will provide students with the knowledge needed to fill the role of worker, citizen, and, someday perhaps, parent.

Assessment should be ongoing and not just at the end of a unit. The purpose of evaluation is to get a snapshot, compared to a previous snapshot, for that individual child. The teacher then knows the strengths and weaknesses of each student and can design further instruction. Tests should determine what students have really learned—not just how well they can interpret. As educators, we need to collect a lot of information from a broad spectrum. The goal is to measure true understanding, not just recall of facts.

As a beginning teacher, it is often difficult to discern between the newest fad and the most effective teaching strategy. However, it is now clear to me that there is something more important than attempting to discover which instructional strategy will be the magical cure. What we, both new teachers and seasoned veterans, need to remember is that <u>our teacher attitudes</u> have a profound impact on students' perceptions, academic behavior, self-concepts, and beliefs. Be mindful of that truth at all times during your career in education.

I wish you all the best as you begin your journey in the education profession. Relish every moment, and use each of those moments as a valuable lesson learned!

Sincerely yours,
Glenda Jones

Dear Young, Naïve, Inexperienced, Caroline,

Anything you can do, I can do better. No offense or anything, I just have so much more experience than you. OK, OK, technically I only have one year under my belt, but it is unbelievable how much you will learn this coming year! You are a hard worker and are always eager to take on new challenges, so this will be fun for you. Don't think it's all rainbows and butterflies, though. You will have to put in a lot of work during the school day and at home this first year. Lucky for you, I have plenty of advice to give.

Don't be nervous! High school students can smell fear. Be consistent, stern, humorous, understanding, caring, but most of all, *be yourself*. You know the material, and you know how to explain it, so let loose! Let the students know that you care about their learning and about their well-being. Be ready for the students to test you, because they will. You will not have a problem overcoming their attempts.

Make sure to stay flexible. In science, new discoveries are made every day. It is vital that you keep up with the times. Also, methods of teaching and school protocols change almost daily. Do not be scared to try new things. Most of the methods are definitely worth a try. Go ahead and sign up for one of the institutes for science teachers offered by one of the state's universities. It is amazing! Go to as many professional development workshops as you can. Make a point of asking your lead teacher for more information on these.

Make sure you write all of your logins and passwords down and save them. By the end of the year, you could quite possibly have a whole notebook full. The worst part about having so many is that each website you are required to be a part of will have different regulations for your password. This makes it ultimately impossible to remember them all. I'm sure you already have a notebook in mind, and I'm positive it will be monogrammed. I know you so well, right?

Do not feel like you don't have a voice. I understand, you are a brand spanking new teacher with no experience and no licensure, but believe me, you are more of a leader than some of the veteran teachers. You are going to hear this from your principal a million times, but it is the solid truth, "Some teachers have one year of experience, and some have twenty years of one year of experience." Keep that in mind.

Another word of wisdom from your principal, "Do not hang out in the teachers' lounge." Now, don't take that literally. You can use the teacher's lounge bathroom, check your mailbox, eat lunch, or even use the copier, but do not go in there to gossip with the other teachers. Your county is a place where everybody knows everybody's business, you know that. Make sure you do not become a part of this, especially when the subject of who will be the softball coach comes up. You know you will be chosen, but until it is announced, you should keep your lips zipped.

Also, it is impossible to start off being lenient on your students and then try to be tough. Make sure you start off stern. Do not bully your students, and do not try to scare them. Let your students know that you mean business. It is important to gain their trust. You can do this by staying consistent. Be respectful and fair to each student. Outside of class, you can act as a mentor to students. Get to know them. They like that. The instant a student is disrespectful, write him or her up. Make sure the students know that bad behavior will not be tolerated in your class.

Sometimes it is hard for a young person to become a respected teacher. The students know you are young and inexperienced. Make sure they know from the start that being flirty and saying things out of the way will result in a write up. Just as soon as it happens for the first time, pull the student who made the comment to the side and talk to him. Just a heads up, this student wants you to go to prom with him. As the saying goes, boys will be boys . . . sweaty, smelly, hormone enraged, boys. However, that does not mean that it is OK for them to treat you that way. You are a professional, and that is the way they need to treat you.

Lastly, remember that you are a beginning teacher, you won't know everything, and you have a lot to learn. I have no doubt in my mind that you will give it your all. Use all of the resources possible and attend as many professional development conferences as possible. Anything you can do to better yourself as a teacher and give you new ideas about teaching STEM, you should do it. Do not feel too overwhelmed. Even if you feel a million miles behind, you are probably not that much behind. I know you well enough to know when you are exaggerating. However, if you do become overwhelmed, make a list and follow it. Making the list, start with the things with the highest priority, and write in descending order until you are finished. Do not worry; the year is going to fly by. Before you know it, you will be in my time, and I'll be a "BT3" (Beginning Teacher, 3rd year).

Experience comes with time, but you can become wiser by taking good advice and learning from your mistakes. Reflect on everything you do so that if it doesn't work out the way you wanted, you know what to do to fix that next time. When you're in up over your head, the first thing to do is close your mouth. The musician Pete Seeger stated the difference between education and experience by saying that "*Education is what you learn when you read the fine print and experience is what you get when you don't.*" Become wiser with every experience! You'll be amazed at how much you will learn in just one year of teaching!

Stay Golden, Ponyboy!*
Caroline Newman

*from a character in Hinton, S.E. (1967). *The Outsiders*. New York: Viking Press.

References

Pete Seeger. (n.d.). BrainyQuote.com. Retrieved May 12, 2017, from BrainyQuote.com Web site: https://www.brainyquote.com/quotes/quotes/p/peteseeger598886.html

Dear Charles,

   You are just now starting out on your chosen career in education. I am writing to you from your future so that I can share some of the enlightenment I have acquired over the years with the hope that you will benefit from hearing about the key things I have learned. So, sit back, read on, and absorb!

   Education is a profession that has changed the lives of many individuals, and even to this very day, it is still impacting lives. Nelson Mandela wrote, "Education is the most powerful weapon we can use to change the world." Change is never easy, and often times it is met with resistance. The resistance may come from within or from an outside source, but usually it is needed and beneficial. Education is a profession that is constantly evolving and changing, and we, as educators, must be very adaptable. As a new teacher, you need to remember that the ability to adapt and overcome is a must, because challenges will arise daily. The problems that novice teachers encounter are very great and very real. One critical issue is that there never seems to be enough time to complete your daily tasks. Next, often, teachers feel as if they are stranded on an island by themselves. Student apathy is another issue one will face and must overcome. The last major issue a novice teacher will be faced with is the responsibility of meeting the needs of all their students. Teaching is not an easy profession, but the outcomes produced are great.

   Time is of the essence when it comes to education. New teachers can become overwhelmed with the requirements they must meet. It is crucial for teachers to take time to learn their students' strength and weaknesses. This may be achieved through student observations, parent contacts, reviewing student cumulative folders, and conferencing with other teachers. Keeping a student portfolio to collect data on students from varying resources throughout the school year creates an informed educator who can track the progress of students. They must prepare lessons weekly that provide a variety of activities for their students. One way to handle this is to pair up with another teacher and work collaboratively on lesson plans. Teachers must constantly assess their students to determine mastery of objectives. Assessment does not necessarily mean standardized tests; it could be as simple as an exit slip from the day's lesson. Teachers must constantly reflect upon their teaching techniques and search for alternative strategies when the one used does not work for a particular objective. One way to accomplish this is to keep a journal and reflect at the end of the day on what worked well, what did not work well, and why and how improvements can be made. Novice teachers must search for resources to assist them with their lessons. They should also develop a great rapport with the media specialist and curriculum specialist to take advantage of their vast knowledge of available curriculum resources and how to use technology effectively.

Novice teachers need support from the administration, experienced teachers, parents, and family. Helen Keller wrote, "Alone we can do nothing. Together we can do so much." Beginning teachers need to be encouraged and supported from all stakeholders. Leaving college and stepping into the world of work with no guidance or direction can be terrifying. I vividly recall my first time stepping into a classroom with thirty-plus students. I was nervous, began to sweat, my mouth became extremely dry, and I almost fainted. Anxiety had taken over, but I was so glad I had a seasoned teacher on my team. She talked with me and told me, "Take it one day at a time, it will get better." She told me that her grandparents told her, "Give a man a fish, he eats for a day; teach him how to fish, he eats for a lifetime." Her goal was to make me the best teacher possible, and she refused to allow me to fail. The administrators at my school were phenomenal. They provided me with all the resources I needed and directed me to order any additional materials I felt were necessary. I took the initiative to contact all parents to introduce myself and let them know I was really looking forward to working with their child. I continued staying in contact with the parents throughout the year. Discussing their child's behavior, academics, character, and attendance proved to be very beneficial. My goal was to let the parents know I have their child's best interest in hand. I wanted to capture the parents' hearts and gain their child's trust, while developing a rapport with them. Family is also important for new teachers. They need moral support from their own family.

The next issue I encountered was student apathy. How do I, as a new teacher or the new kid on the block, motivate and inspire my students to learn? Joe Martin wrote, "Student apathy is like kryptonite to an average teacher; but it's a personal challenge to a great one." I knew I had to build on students' interests and align their interests with the mandated curriculum. It was a challenge and a task, but I knew I had to overcome the obstacles. I created assignments that inspired my students to ask questions, explore, explain, and observe. My lessons were designed around inquiry-based and project-based learning. The traditional classroom was boring to the students. They were not motivated or inspired to learn. I moved from a teacher-centered classroom to a student-centered classroom. Instead of my asking the students questions, I wanted the students to ask me questions. I wanted to empower my students and hold them accountable for their own learning. My goal was to provide my students with learning that was enduring.

Lastly, one size does not fit all. As educators, we have the responsibility to meet the needs of all our students. Dr. Gene Carter wrote, "We must meet our students exactly where they are with exactly the brains they have right now. We must use all the tools we have available to us and not expect them to fit into a mold or all behave exactly the same." It is impossible to fit a square inside of a circle, but this is what most teachers are doing, and when students fail, the teacher does not understand why. I know when we teach to the middle, never focusing on the lower or upper end of the spectrum, we are omitting the students who need the most help. Those are the students who are suffering. On the lower end, students are not learning due to the fact that the material is too challenging for them, and for those on the upper end, the material lacks rigor. The majority of teachers lean toward teaching the way they were taught, but students do not learn the way we learned. To reach learners of the 21st century, we need to integrate technology. Teachers can design lessons to meet the needs of all students if they incorporate technology. Technology helps even the shiest child in a classroom learn to share his or her voice. It opens up new opportunities that allow us to connect with other educators and students around the world. Technology helps us pace different students at different points in the learning. It gives us data that we never had before to help us develop individualized plans based on student strengths and weaknesses. We must create students who are self-sustaining citizens and able to function in an ever-changing society. We have no excuses for not meeting the needs of our students.

Teachers have a huge responsibility preparing students for the 21st century, and the beginning teacher has an even a greater accountability. The issues they face can often times seem impossible:

- There is never enough time to finish tasks.
- The paperwork is constantly piling up and incomplete.

- A new initiative has been adopted by the district or the state, and we are charged with attending professional development and being able to carry out effective implementation of the initiative.
- These students are not interested in learning; how can I motivate them?
- Wow, every student is different! I thought they all came out of the same pack.

These are just a few of the issues one will encounter the first year. Remember, I said the first year, because each year will progressively get better. Relationships will develop with other teachers, resources will become more accessible, and knowledge of differentiation of instruction will increase.

Have faith in yourself, and trust that you will learn and grow with each new experience. You have a rewarding future ahead as a teacher and as a school administrator. Hang on for an exciting ride!

All the best from your future self,
Charles Locklear

References

Carter, G.R. (2013, February 14) *Meeting the Needs of Our Students and Educators*, ASCD. Retrieved January 17, 2017, from: http://inservice.ascd.org/meeting-the-needs-of-our-students-and-our-educators/

Keller, H. (n.d.). BrainyQuote.com. Retrieved January 17, 2017, from https://www.brainyquote.com/quotes/quotes/h/helenkelle382259.html

Mandela, N. (n.d.). BrainyQuote.com. Retrieved January 17, 2017, from https://www.brainyquote.com/quotes/quotes/n/nelsonmand157855.html

Martin, J. (n.d.). EducatorMotivatorQuote.com. Retrieved January 17, 2017 from https://305927716147259.offertabs.com/2654671?view=pins&board.

Dear me, a beginning science teacher,

I want you to know I understand that right now you are very scared even though you do not want to show it. Beginning anything new is uncomfortable, but this is especially true in teaching. All those student minds are depending on you as the teacher, and you realize that this is a big responsibility, and of course, you want to do your very best! So my advice is not to be so hard on yourself!

Good teaching is difficult, and it takes time, so give yourself the time. Be reflective, expect to make mistakes, but always learn from them. So, I think what you need to do is to have a plan to learn from your mistakes. Instead of being afraid of mistakes, embrace them, and learn from them. Seek out others to help you with what you struggle with regarding teaching. Ask other teachers specific questions, and they will be happy to help.

Trust yourself and your intuition instead of always second guessing yourself. I know that you know that you are the teacher, so you really do know a lot about what is best for your students. However, when an administrator tells you to do something, then try and do it. Do not be offended, because he or she is trying to help you to be the best teacher possible for students. My assistant principal told me two years in a row to smile more. I was offended and hurt by the comment. I was confused, too. I asked him for clarification and still did not understand what he was trying to tell me. I get it now, though. He was saying to me to relax, have fun, and to enjoy the time I have with my students. Enjoying means laughing, looking for teachable moments, and listening carefully to the students and what they would like me to teach them and how. So, do enjoy your students and have fun! Embrace what is so special about them.

The great thing about becoming a teacher that I wish someone would have told me, that I am now telling you, is that you will learn as much about yourself as you will learn about your students and how to teach. Being a teacher is deeply personal. My husband told me that I do not have a job; instead, I have a career. But he was wrong. Being a teacher is much more than a career. Instead it is WHO I AM! I want you to be proud and confident of the fact that you are a teacher. Embrace this and the moment. Be proud of it, and do not let others belittle who you are—A TEACHER! I am a better person as the result of being a teacher. I changed my students, but my students changed me even more! Be proud of who you are—*always*!

Being a science teacher is especially challenging, so I want you to take your time and to add new ideas and techniques slowly. I know that you want to be like that great experienced teacher down the hall, but it is not going to happen in one year, two years, or even in five years. It takes time to learn all the tricks that an experienced teacher knows. But you can and will learn over time by observing, asking questions, and taking notes every chance you can from every experienced teacher you meet. Identify your own weaknesses through reflections and based on feedback from others. Then, you need to find an experienced teacher who has figured it out. Learning from them how to improve your own teaching is what is most important. Teaching is all about constantly learning through reflection over time. Do try experiments, but not so many new experiments at the same time. This will just drive you crazy and be frustrating. Do add a few experiments at a time, and when you feel comfortable with those, try other projects, activities, and experiments as well. Learning how to organize a lab and equipment and how to find funding for what you need to buy will take time. So, I am telling you that it is okay to give yourself that time.

Another thing that you need to remember is that parents are on your side, just like administrators. Please do talk to parents about their children and talk to them often. Be positive and celebrate successes. It is much more fun than focusing on the negatives. Find ways to involve parents in their child's education. This is much more difficult at the secondary level, but it results in huge benefits for you as the teacher and for your students. The extra time is truly worth it. It took me a long time to realize this, so start early to collaborate with parents, just like you should with administrators.

Finally, I want to tell you, as a former beginning teacher myself, to focus on the big things mentioned above. Put them into your professional life first, and forget and let go of all those small things, like the noisy desks or the pencil sharpener that just will not work! Relax and enjoy *THE INCREDIBLE JOURNEY CALLED TEACHING*. It is truly a once in a lifetime opportunity and an honor. It changed my life and my destiny forever, and I know that will be true for you, too.

I understand what you are going through now. I'm here for you, so call on me if you need me.

Wishing you the best always,
Rita Hagevik

Dear Dave,

This is your first year of teaching, and you are full of ideas, and you are eager to change the world by making the lives of others better through educating the youth of tomorrow. Education is a lot different today than it was when you were a boy growing up in rural Maryland. Students have more distractions today than when you were in middle school, but remember that they are still kids. Even though the world around them has changed, the kid inside them has not. They have the same interests and behavior. Kids have not changed, but we as adults have. As a teacher, it is your job to open the world of science to your students and make it real to them.

Your first year will be challenging, but hang in there because it will be rewarding. The students that you will teach will bring you lots of pride, both academically and as athletes. You will have a student who ends up playing for a college team that wins the National Championship, and you will have students who succeed in high school and college. At the time of this letter, the oldest students that you have taught are still in college, but they have very bright futures ahead of them. It's important that you do not get discouraged; you will influence many students who will touch the lives of thousands. Your students will become doctors, lawyers, educators, engineers, and, most importantly, parents with their own families. I want to tell you that the students you teach each year are not the reason you continue to teach; rather, it is the ones who come back years later thanking you for all that you have done for them.

As a teacher, you are a lifetime learner. You need to be an example to your students. They will watch you and follow your progress as you return to graduate school to further your education. Be enthusiastic and respect your students. I have found this to be the key to our success over the years. If you respect your students, they will work hard for you, and they will do their best not to let you down.

As a personal note, you will be cut after your first year of teaching due to budget constraints, and even though this will be a stressful time, it will be the best thing to happen to you. You will end up at a little school in a rural county, and you will excel there. You will become the department chair, and you will have opportunities that you would not have received at a larger school in a large county. You will be sponsored to attend the National Science Teachers Association's national convention, and you will return to school inspired. My advice to you is to get involved with your school, community, and students. Start extracurricular activities and clubs. These activities will help increase your students' interest in science, and the response for membership in these clubs will be overwhelming.

As a teacher, you want to engage your students. You started out believing in activities that encouraged hands-on learning, and you need to continue using this powerful teaching philosophy. Your students will make real-world connections to the science content that you will teach. You will be exposed to student data, and you will be using this data to drive your teaching; but remember not to lose the personal connection to your students. They are kids and not a number in the data bank.

Your students will know that you love what you teach, and they will respond to this positively. To help enhance your teaching, it is important to incorporate field trips into your lesson plans. Students will retain content when they can put a visual picture to the content that you are teaching. Your first field trip will be to the ocean. You need to take this field trip because on this specific trip, you had a student tell you that they have never seen the ocean before, even though they have lived an hour from the coast their whole life. This brings up my next point.

The second school that you will teach at is a very poor school in a very poor county. Please encourage your students, and let them know that they can do whatever they put their mind to. These students will be the best students that you have taught during your nine years of teaching. You will have among the highest test scores in the county in which you are teaching, and the leadership you have exhibited will pay off.

The legacy that you will leave behind will be your students. Through your life, you will touch hundreds of students, who in turn will touch thousands of individuals. Dave, you started teaching in order to change the world, and to make the lives of others better—and you have! Enjoy each day with your students. You are changing the world through your students!

From your future,
Dave Wimert

My dearest Corinne,

So, you did it! You have opened the door to one of the most rewarding careers. Finally, college and graduate school is over. Corinne, you must feel a sense of relief that all the studying is over, and now it is time for your work life to start. Now, I am sure you can almost reminisce on all the wise words and advice everyone has and is giving you on how to handle the first year of teaching.

Are you thinking about the first day of school, facing a sea of faces all looking at you waiting for your first words to them? No matter what, you can always rely on your own experiences when you were at school. Is this true? Maybe, if you hadn't experienced high school in another country. What are schools in America like? Do students stand up when another teacher enters the room? Are teachers respected, and do behaviors have consequences? Corinne, you are in for a learning curve, too.

One of the biggest challenges as a new teacher is establishing classroom rules and procedures. These need to be established from the first day of school.

You may ask, "How do I set rules and procedures when I am a first-year teacher?" The answer to this is complicated. You need to ask another teacher for an example that could be adapted to your classroom. As you proceed through your first semester, make notes about what worked and didn't work, and make the necessary changes the next time. The vital thing is that from the first day you need to establish your rules so that all students know what is expected from them, and they must know that certain behaviors will result in consequences. Too many times there have been stories of teachers who leave after a day or week or so. They have probably not succeeded in this.

A method that assists with student behavior is assigned seating. When students have assigned seats from the beginning of the year, this helps them to understand that you are the leader of that classroom, and it helps you to learn the names of your students. This helps to establish a personal relationship with each student, which in turn will create a mutual respect that is important to foster a positive, learning environment that minimizes behavioral problems. Be prepared to change these seating arrangements as you observe certain positive or negative student interactions with each other.

A mutual respect and positive relationship between you and your students will assist in diffusing or even avoiding potential conflicts. You will have a student (or a few) who has proven behavioral problems; however, the positive and respectful attitude that you show will win these students over. Young people need to feel you care and need the structure that you provide in your room.

The second challenge you will face is lesson planning. Make sure you spend considerable time and efforts in planning. Your efforts will reduce time and stress on you for your future semesters. Also, as you plan, make sure you organize all electronic and paper files very efficiently to ensure the smooth flow of your daily routines the next time you teach the course. Be aware that this is tiring and cumbersome, but it does pay off in the long run. The second most time-consuming activity will be grading. To assist yourself with this task, use electronic resources that will aid in accelerating your grading process. Another method that can be used to speed up the grading process is to have students grade each other's projects. This can serve two purposes. Firstly, it helps to free up a little of your after-school time, and secondly, it allows students the opportunity to analyze and critique the work of others. Young people like to feel a sense of responsibility, and this necessitates a certain amount of reinforcement of the content taught.

As a beginning teacher, you will spend a considerable amount of time in your lesson planning. It is very important that you also take time for yourself. There need to be times where you pack all work away and relax and do something for yourself. This is essential to prevent burnout.

Another helpful hint is to get to know your colleagues and the administration at your school. There will be days that you feel alone and overwhelmed. It is very easy to get caught up in these feelings and not reach out for help. This is the best advice I could ever give you. Ask as many people you meet as possible, and you will find all the help you need. I remember back near the beginning of the year, I was feeling very overwhelmed and stressed. It was lunch time, and I walked out to the courtyard and saw an administrator who greeted me kindly. Then I found myself telling him all about it. Much to my surprise, he offered to help and offered suggestions on how I could solve these issues I was having. Six months later, I had a meeting with this administrator, and he said to me "I knew you were going to be an excellent teacher since you reached out and asked for help."

A challenge of all teachers is what teaching strategies to use to not only teach, but teach effectively. There are many possibilities, and there are many courses and books on this. Knowledge is power with regard to effective teaching strategies, and there is no better way to determine what works than to try them out yourself. Something often overlooked is the necessity to change your teaching strategies, even in one single lesson. Students cannot concentrate for long periods of time on a given task. They need information shortened and compartmentalized, and they often need hands-on activities following any lecture material. Furthermore, all class activities need to be timed. Students are far more likely to complete tasks if they know what their deadline is. Remember that technology is something that is strongly suggested to be integrated in your classes. There are so many useful teacher websites and applications that you can use in your teaching.

The use of cellular devices and school-issued laptops by students is exploding and will be a common issue that you must deal with. There is no single solution for this, but the secret is to determine your policy on each and to reinforce it every day. Students are easily distracted by incoming texts, taking pictures, and the lure of the Internet, and you need to establish an electronic policy in order for them to stay on task.

They say nobody stops learning. You learn about yourself everyday—as a person, as a leader, and as a teacher. No matter how much advice you receive, there is no substitute for experience, and your teaching will adapt and grow as you go along. Most importantly, be yourself in your classroom. Remember that you are unique, with a dynamic personality of your own. Don't be afraid of being YOU! Don't let a fear of coming from a diverse cultural background discourage you. This is to your benefit and not a disadvantage. USE IT! If you pronounce a word differently, your students will most likely remember it longer. Most of all, never forget to have a good laugh—both with the class and at yourself!

Stay awesome!

Your future self,
Corinne Jordan

April 4, 2017

Dear Shane,

It's too late to say, "Run the other way!" You've gone-and-done-it now! You know Daddy said you did not want to go into teaching, and he ought to know since he recently retired just before you started your jump into education. Of course, he's going to tell you he "doesn't really want to hear you whine and complain about it," but secretly he's proud of you anyway. *(I know this now because he traveled to see you graduate with your PhD, even though he was weak and gravely sick.)* Grandma Nita is a completely different story. She so believes you have answered your calling in life that she'll financially help you in reaching your highest academic goals, and one day, you'll find you've lived out the dream she had for herself, but never did see fulfilled.

I do have some well-intentioned words of advice I would like to share with you from the perspective I now have after completing 16 years of teaching, earning National Board Certification as a Middle Childhood Generalist, completing a Master's of Education in Reading, and obtaining a Doctorate of Philosophy in Curriculum and Instruction in Literacy. I'm not sharing all those things to brag, but to show you that you will one day accomplish your goals as you persevere through the coming years. I'm also not going to share what difficulties you endured, because I know that today I am who and what I am because of the way I weathered those times, and I don't want you to change course; however, there are some points I want to share with you to perhaps make the coming seasons more effective and fulfilling.

1. Learn to take a breath before you speak your frustrations with difficult students and irritating classes. You can accomplish more with a whisper than a shout. *(I'm still working on this one!!!)*

2. Take the time to recognize the students who don't stand out in the forefront of class activities. Make a mental note to call their name, or to give a high-five, or to just talk to them. I want you to feel confident at the end of the day you had spoken and acknowledged every student.

3. You will spend your entire career after this first year in sixth grade. Think back to your sixth grade year and how special Mrs. T. was to you and be that kind of teacher along the way to your students. There will be hard times, attitudes galore, and moments you will be tempted to change grades, but you

will find a joy in the wonder of childhood that is still strong in these 11–13 year-old students. Pursue that notion and use it to engage their excitement about life and about becoming.

4. God blessed you with the ability to relate to children, and it is in those relationships you develop with students where you will challenge, motivate, and engage learners to do great things. The ballgames, cheerleading competitions, band performances (which will prompt you to call your mother every year to say, "Thanks Mom, for enduring that first year of band when I was in sixth grade!"), dances, and football games you go to will mean more than you can possibly imagine to your students, parents, grandparents, and community members who will be watching you along the way.

5. Play soccer earlier! You will love the game, and it will become a passion that you could enjoy for more years than I have been able to. It will also help you develop stronger relationships with your Hispanic students, and there will be many of those; and if you play, others who would normally sit on the sidelines without being engaged in other sports will get engaged and develop multiethnic, multigendered, and multifaceted relationships. Don't neglect to spend time with the other students who have interests in traditional sports, but I promise soccer is something you will love.

6. Learn to speak Spanish as quickly as you can! You will build bridges and help students and their families more quickly adjust to life in your school's community. The relationships you build with some of your Hispanic students

will be the warmest relationships you will have, and how much richer those would be, if you learn to communicate in their language.

7. Take time to honor and work to develop relationships with the Lumbee tribe. You will find a special joy in working in a school that is majority American Indian. Pay attention to the special stories the students share at lunch with you and with each other in your hearing. One day those stories will provide you fertile ground to write. There will be a passion that develops to reach out and to embrace and understand the local culture, and the relationships that develop from that pursuit will be lifelong. There's a home-away-from-home environment that will grow from those experiences, and the sooner you recognize that, the more you can enrich your life and the local community.

I have so many thoughts to share with you, but for now, I hope these nuggets of gradually attained wisdom will start you out on the right path. Utilizing this advice will greatly improve the coming years, and it will help you to find even more fulfillment and joy in the career you've chosen. I know it's difficult to look into the future from where you stand now, but—*TRUST ME ON THIS*—if you incorporate these ideas into your teaching practice, you will find your days to be much richer, and, when you look back, you will be pleased with the teacher you will become!

Sincerely,
Your voice to come,
(Michael) Shane Fletcher

Dear Younger Self,

When you step into the classroom, twenty-plus eighth graders will look to you as a source of knowledge, as if you hold all the answers. You already know that you don't know it all, and you're not afraid to admit it. Some teachers act as if they know it all, and their students, especially middle school students, will probe them with questions just to knock them off their high horse. Those are the teachers that students don't care to listen to because no one likes a know-it-all. They will listen to you, though, because from day one you have shown that you care. A future administrator will affix this famous quote to every weekly bulletin for the entire school year, "Students don't care how much you know until they know how much you care." Over the years, you will find this to be true. Lucky for you, caring comes naturally for you. You show you care by greeting them each morning with a smile and calling them by name. You show them you care by asking about their basketball game or about their ballet recital. For you, it's simple because you were born to be a teacher. You are a teacher who is still learning each day.

The truth is, you will learn along with them, and you will never stop being a student. After a few months in the classroom, you realize this is what you were born to do. In a few years, you go back to school to get your Master's, then on to obtain National Board Certification. Yeah, you do that! You learn so much over the years. A lot of what you learn, though, isn't what you learned in college. You didn't learn how deal with the young girl who lost her mother last school year. She sits and doodles messages and letters to her mom when she should be working. You didn't learn to deal with the young boy who carries around anger because his home life is so bad. He lashes out at others because it's the only way he knows to communicate. You care for them and look for ways to help them learn. You learn what works for them. You learn that writing for the young girl is cathartic and helps her cope with her mother's death. You learn that the young boy is very intelligent and reads well, but nobody ever noticed it because he was quickly dismissed because of his anger issues. You introduce him to the Bluford Series novels because he can relate to the themes, and a lot of what he reads mirrors his own life. He uses reading as an escape just as the young girl uses her writing. You learn this in the classroom with your students. You learn about them and with them.

It will take you a few years to figure things out when it comes to teaching your content, but here's a heads up on some great practices you need to go ahead and start implementing in your classroom. You must do all these for your students to benefit now and in the future. Just trust me on this; I have quite a bit of experience.

Despite popular belief, a quiet classroom is not the best classroom, unless everyone is silently reading, of course. A classroom that is full of academic discourse is best for learning. Give your students the opportunity to discuss what they've read, facilitate discussions, and let them have debates and Socratic Seminars. If you don't know what I'm talking about it, Google it. Also, teach them to write, and teach them grammar. They will appreciate this when they get to college; their college instructors will appreciate it as well. You will actually have students visit you once they get to college and thank you for teaching them to write that five paragraph essay. Give your students time to read books they enjoy while you read, also. Nurture a love for reading, and let them see that you love to read, too. Share with them what you're reading, and they will see the fire in your eyes, and they may think you're crazy, but they will never forget it.

Don't stress about the things you can't change. You will disagree with certain administrative decisions or district policies, but learn to focus on your students and your classroom. For example, your district's pacing guide is a guide; it's not the Bible for teaching. Of course, you need to teach the standards, but how you teach it and when will be based upon the group of students you're teaching. Get to know your students, what they know, how they learn, then go from there. It sounds easy, but it's not. It will take time, and it will be exhausting, but it will be worth it. You're gonna figure it out!

I do have to mention one more ridiculous thing you do that you need to stop doing immediately! Stop taking that bag home … Yeah, you know, the one with all the papers that you say you're going to grade, but never get around to. You are literally hauling papers back and forth. It's crazy. Manage your time wisely during the school day and stay over about 30 minutes each day, so you don't have to worry about grading papers on the weekend. Besides, family time is what keeps you grounded. Your weekend time is the fuel you need to prepare for another week. Don't forsake your family for your job. Don't get so caught up in caring about your kids at school that you don't have time or energy for your own kids. When you teach with your heart, it's physically, emotionally, and mentally exhausting. At the end of the day, let it all go, and go home. Just make sure at the end of the day you can say you did your best. It may not seem like it, but within the four walls of that classroom, you are changing the world.

Sincerely,
Someone who needed reminding of why she teaches,
Latisha Sullivan

Dear bright-eyed, first-year teacher,

The big day is finally here! I imagine you have picked out a first-day-of-school outfit, your lunch is packed, and your teacher bag is ready. Enjoy this moment of preparedness, because you are embarking on a rollercoaster ride that can't be described until you experience it yourself!

You are entering the most noble of professions. Seriously, it is likely the MOST IMPORTANT JOB OF ALL! You are idealistic and think you can change the world. Don't let the naysayers in the teacher workroom discourage you when they tell you to be realistic. One student at a time, you will change the world for the better.

When you face your class for the first time, don't be surprised if your voice shakes and your hands tremble. This is a big deal, and things get real when you look into the eyes of your very first group of students. You've been preparing for this moment since you played school with your stuffed animals. Really focus on your students. If you put what is best for them in the forefront of every decision you make, you will be successful, and so will they.

When you get your first paycheck, you will probably run to the school treasurer, telling her there has been a big mistake and your salary, divided by 12, should be much more than the amount you see on your check. There are other professions you could have chosen that are more financially rewarding, but none that will make your heart so full. It's true that a full heart won't pay your bills, so budget wisely, and when the financial advisors visit your school with information about retirement and savings, listen carefully and save as much as you can.

Pick your battles. If a student doesn't bring a pencil to class, just give them one. Be fair and consistent when enforcing your class rules, but remember that your students are human beings and that we all have bad days. Start each day with a clean slate. Students shouldn't be defined by their bad days, but by the potential they have to grow and improve. Help them reach that potential.

One day, you will attend graduation ceremonies and weddings of the students you have in this very first class. You will never, ever, ever forget them. They will always hold a place in your heart. But make room for more, because there are hundreds yet to come.

With love,
The Future You,
Tierney Fairchild

Dearest twenty-two-year-old excited and enthusiastic beginning teacher—Martha,

Trying to imagine the magnitude of memorable experiences you will have over the thirty-six years you spend in public education is nearly impossible. You will work in four different counties in five schools under the supervision of ten principals. Along the way you will work in two condemned buildings and one with an open-classroom design. The last six years of your career will be spent working for a state department of education as a regional facilitator, working closely with a dozen or more school districts. The time will fly and the children and colleagues you meet along the way will leave a lasting impression on your heart for the rest of your life. You will receive several awards: "Honor Teacher" designation from the university you attended and "Teacher of the Year" from your school, county, and region. You will also achieve and renew your National Board for Professional Teaching Standards certification.

I share this information about your later accomplishments because I want you to know that you will have a successful career in education. I clearly remember that the first few years are overwhelming, and you will want to ask for your parents' money back from your college because you feel unprepared for the daunting task that is teaching. But, you will survive with the help of many colleagues. Leaning on them is important. Model yourself after the ones who do their job well daily. You will learn as much about yourself as your students learn about life and the world around them. You have chosen one of the most noble of professions. The impact you'll have on your students will be your legacy. Please take it seriously and learn from your mistakes. You will make them, but grow from them.

There are so many memories that will flood your thoughts from year to year, like the time a teacher tells you that you expect too much from your students. Although you are taken aback by the statement, you remark, "Well, if I expect too much from them, then maybe they will give me what they really can do." The impact that statement has on your first year in the classroom causes you to make a career decision. You decide that all children, regardless of their ethnicity or socio-economic background, can and will learn from you. From that point forward, this is the way you conduct your class. "*High expectations equal results*" is your mantra, and it works for you. You hold your students accountable for their work, often to the chagrin of the children and the parents, but it always pays off in the end, and many times the children and parents come back to you to thank you for what you did for them.

Over the years, you will refine your approach to teaching. Your first principal has words of wisdom that have merit as time passes. For example, he talks to you about how your opinion about homework will change when you have children of your own, and it definitely does. He listens when you return from a professional development conference and you share what you learned. He smiles, looks at you and says, "Anderson, everything in education is circular. There's nothing new; they just call it something different." Over the years you realize that, for the most part, it's true. There are many things about education that are basic requirements of learning and need to be taught. The change comes from the way you teach, learning to differentiate your instruction to meet the needs of the individual students and not simply teach whole group all day. You will move away from worksheets and basal textbooks, to creating your own materials based on the novels your students read. You will become known as the "project queen" because for every novel your students read, there is a literature extension project that is assigned, as well as a social studies or science project that addresses the objectives of the units you teach. You encourage parents to assist students with the projects because you feel it's important for children to learn what a quality product is. Your hope is that when they are able to complete a project on their own, they will create quality work throughout their school years, but more importantly, for the remainder of their lives.

Speaking of life, you spend time talking to your students about real life, touting the pros of education and how important it is for reaching their "when-I-grow-up" goals. There will be many children and parents who will need these "come-to-Jesus" talks over the years, and you do not take that responsibility lightly. You believe that educating the children with life skills is as important as their academic education. You also believe that identifying the strengths of students, focusing as much attention to those attributes as you do to their areas of concern, is important to their lifelong learning.

For your entire career, the children are the single most important reason you get up every morning to go to school early so you can be prepared when they come through the door. The first day of each year is when you lay the foundation for the next 179 days. You talk to your students about your expectations, your classroom management system and discipline plan, and you make it a point to learn each student's name and something about them within the first hour of the morning. Your classroom expectations are simple:

> *Be prepared for school;*
>
> *Be respectful of others, their property, and the school's property;*
>
> *Be your best self every day; and*
>
> *No matter what, Mrs. A is always right.*

The students love the last expectation, and it will end many discussions quickly. You are the *Queen* of your classroom and everyone understands this, even your colleagues. Your philosophy is: *Outside of the four walls of your classroom is a democracy, but inside it's a monarchy, and I am the **Queen**.* This may sound harsh, but over time, you come to realize that it all rests on your shoulders. You may have others who assist you, but ultimately, all the responsibility for those children entrusted to you lies solely with you. You are the one who will answer to parents and administrators for the job you do or don't do.

One idea that has a tremendous impact on your classroom management is the use of soft drink cans, Coke and Mtn Dew. I know, it sounds ridiculous, but trust me, it works like a charm! On the first day of school, you explain to your students that when they arrive in the mornings, if a Coke is sitting on your desk, then it's a good day. They can come into the classroom and speak to one another, unpack, and get busy on their morning assignments. However, if a Mtn Dew is on your desk, they need to come in quietly with no talking, unpack, and start their morning work. You further explain the Mtn Dew means it's not a good morning for you, and it's important for them to be as quiet as possible. This is the GREATEST idea you will ever have in managing the behaviors in your classroom! The funniest example of this is when you put the Coke on your desk for six days in a row, and on the seventh day, you decide to put the Mtn Dew can out, for no particular reason. The children are coming down the hall to the classroom, and suddenly the first boy stops, and it creates a multi-collision of students reminiscent of a cartoon. The first boy turns around and looks at the rest of the class and says silently and demonstratively, "MOUNTAIN DEW, MOUNTAIN DEW!" Immediately, total silence befalls the group, and they enter the room quietly, even trying to unzip their book bags and sharpen pencils with little to no sound. It's all you can do not to laugh out loud and ruin the whole premise of the cans. Years later, you see several boys from this class in a fast food restaurant, and they ask you if it's a Coke or Mtn Dew day. You laugh and say, "It's definitely a Coke day," as you plop down at their table to chat for a few minutes about their lives now. Who would ever think that using a Coke or Mtn Dew could transform your approach to classroom management? This simple idea changes who you are in the classroom. You go from someone who raises your voice to control the classroom to someone who rarely needs to raise your voice at all. Maybe you owe some kind of royalty to the soft drink franchises, who knows? But, if so, it's worth every penny.

As I mentioned before, the students are the number one reason why you continue to remain in the classroom for thirty years. You believe that children should be *loved*, *nurtured*, and then *educated*, in that order. Every year there's a new group of students who become your children for life. You love all of them, but there are some that will stand out to you over your career. You have this uncanny ability to relate to boys, especially those who exhibit risky behaviors. Each year there's a child that you feel drawn to because, up to this point, his school career has not been positive. Here's one that comes to mind. His name is JT. When he walks into your classroom, you know he is the "leader" among the class. It's important to win him over quickly. You have to establish yourself as the alpha in the room. Remember, you're the **Queen**. You recognize that he is one of the smartest boys you've taught, but his anger gets in his way. He pushes you to your limits on many days, but you never give up on him. You talk to him on a daily basis about not letting his anger derail his potential to graduate and go to college. Working closely with his mother, you demand his best, and although he resists more than you like, by the end of the year, the relationship you develop will last for years to come. Fast forward several years to the day you're in the grocery store and you see his mother. You learn that JT is now a junior in college. You are thrilled. After the pleasantries are over and his mother walks away, she returns and, with phone in hand, tells the person on the other end there's someone who wants to speak to him. She hands you the phone and you say, "Hey, JT! Do you know who this is?" He says, "Say my name again." You do, and he immediately says, "Mrs. Anderson, is that you?" The two of you talk for several minutes. He's working on a double major, Criminal Justice and Philosophy. How great is that? This child, because of his anger, could have easily ended up on the opposite side of the criminal justice system, and now he is choosing this as a career. As you say good-bye, you tell him you love him, and he says, "Mrs. Anderson, I love you, too." There are no words to explain the joy you feel at that moment. This will happen over the years with numerous children. Many will attend college and have successful careers and build beautiful families. Some will be outstanding athletes and will receive scholarships to play at the college level. Unfortunately, there are students you work so hard with, but it doesn't turn out as positively. There will be students who end up on the opposite side of the law, and your heart will break for them. You are like a parent to your students, and to have just one child who struggles with life fills your heart with sadness.

As you begin this journey, know there will be times of trials and tribulations as well as joys and celebrations. I can promise you the celebrations will outweigh the difficult times. It is said that in their first year of teaching, new teachers experience several phases that include *anticipation*, *survival*, *disillusionment*, *rejuvenation*, and *reflection* (New Teacher Center, 2011). Sometimes that first year feels like you are on a roller coaster ride! I need you to know that ALL teachers feel this way, but those who remain in the classroom know that it is possible to navigate your way through those phases. Teaching is a calling, and you are called to be a teacher. There will be times you tread water, barely keeping your head up, but other times you will be able to swim like an Olympic champion. Don't be afraid to jump in the pool. I have faith in you. ***You can do this!***

Wishing you courage and perseverance for this wonderful journey,
Your thirty-six-year veteran and now happily retired self—Martha Anderson
Copyright © Martha Anderson. Reprinted by permission.

Reference

New Teacher Center. (2011). *Phases of First-Year Teaching* (retrieved May 7, 2017 from https://newteachercenter.org/blog/2011/08/17/phases-of-first-year-teaching/)

Letters Written to Novice Teachers in Specialty Areas

"Life is a succession of lessons which must be lived to be understood."

Ralph Waldo Emerson (1803–1882), U.S. essayist, poet, philosopher, in "Illusions," <u>The Conduct of Life</u> (1860).

HI Miss ROACH!!!

I hope this correspondence finds you doing well. I am curious—Do your students pick on you about your last name? Probably not the best teacher name to have, but I am sure it is definitely a good icebreaker when you interact with new students. And if I know you, you have probably laughed off any insult or given some creative response to a teasing word.

At any rate, I just wanted to take a few minutes to tell you that I am so glad that you followed your heart and your passion! It was not by chance . . . As your mother taught you how to read in the basement of military housing, you dreamed of one day becoming a teacher. It was not by chance . . . As you proudly wrote "I want to be a teacher" when asked in second grade the question, "What do you want to be when you grow up?" And it certainly was not by chance that as a fourth grader, you absolutely fell in love with individuals with disabilities while attending Special Olympics with your dad. *Becoming a teacher—a special education teacher—has always been inside of you.*

I am so proud of how you worked to bring excellence into every facet of your teaching. The way in which you would prepare throughout the months of June and July to ensure that all your materials were ready to go in August definitely reflected that. The way you arrived a few days before teachers were required to return did not go unnoticed. Often times, the custodians would thank you for "beating the rush" and allowing them to put down carpets, arrange desks, and lift bookcases in a more relaxed fashion. As a new teacher, you were not afraid to seek resources and advocate for the students with disabilities in your class. As a K-5 Special Education teacher, you attended each grade level meeting to ensure that *YOUR* students (because you loved each one of those boys and girls as if they were your own) had the resources, opportunities, and materials needed to succeed. And you can imagine how many meetings you attended each month! But through your advocacy, your students were included within more grade level activities, such as assemblies, field trips, and awards, than they had in previous years. The principal once commented on how "you had not let your light hide under a bushel barrel," meaning, you made students, who many try to make invisible, a vital part of the school community. You helped to educate your colleagues on the needs of your students and partnered within to maximize the success of all children, including your students with disabilities.

You were not afraid to challenge and empower students who many thought could not learn. As a new teacher, you were innovative as you integrated what you had learned in college into the daily lessons for your students. In fact, you used several activities that were course requirements within the learning centers in your classroom. You were never one to let a good idea go to waste!!

You utilized your teaching assistants as vital members of your classroom. They could be observed assisting and interacting with small groups of students. In your eyes, any adult in your classroom was an educator, so no hands ever sat idle. There was always someone to be taught, and you created that type of environment. It was a good thing that you did, because many of your colleagues didn't really think that you "taught." They thought your students just sat around and watched videos and played all day. You helped to reshape some general educators' views on educational programming for students with disabilities.

You recognized that an effective teacher is one who knows, respects, and appreciates her students and their families. Thus, you read each Individualized Education Plan (IEP) to determine the child's strengths as well as his or her areas in need of improvement, and you worked to weave each of these components into the lessons that you planned. You used what your students knew and loved to motivate them to learn new concepts. You recognized the uniqueness of each child and celebrated his or her individuality. When you discovered one of your students needed to have the same daily routine, even if he checked into school late, you made sure he had breakfast waiting at 11:00 am when he arrived. You called each family prior to the school year beginning, just to introduce yourself and chat about their child; and for many parents that was the first time that a teacher had ever called without having anything bad to say about their child. When you wanted parents or guardians to attend events—such as an annual arts festival, teacher conferences, awards ceremony, you name it—you made sure to give them at least three weeks, if not more, advanced notice. You recognized that many of your parents worked jobs that required at least two weeks' notice in order to take any leave time. And I tell you, when anyone looked into the audience, your students had 100% parental participation at quite a few events!

You listened to the parents' concerns and always made sure that their voice was heard at any meeting concerning their child. You discussed things so they could understand the professional jargon and truly know what was being decided upon for their son or daughter.

You were the poster child for a lifelong learner. Any and every professional development opportunity, you were there! You had some difficulties saying "no," but I can see now that each of those opportunities helped to enhance some critical aspect of your professional development.

You learned to balance the paperwork demands of the job by creating a file folder system where all the information for every child was tracked, stored, and kept organized. Because you did not have a planning period, you often stayed late to grade papers, plan various learning centers, and complete IEP forms. But you never complained, because you recognized that this sacrifice of time would greatly help you in the long run. You were able to submit required paperwork, assessments, lesson plans, and reports on time.

You have made a difference in so many children's lives because you stayed true to yourself and lived your dream out loud . . . each and every day. You allowed your good days to outweigh the bad, you took it one day at time, one lesson at a time—and you stayed in it for the children . . . *YOUR* children! You worked within a team to help each individual child reach his or her potential, his or her fullest potential.

Words cannot truly express how proud of you I am! Please don't ever lose that passion. You may need it one day—when you decided to teach pre-service special educators. They will need to see that light shine brightly in your eyes as you use illustrations from your time in a K-8 classroom.

Yours in the Profession,
MDRS (Marisa Roach Scott)

Dear Yours Hapless Novice,

So, you've decided that you want to be a special education teacher. I know that your schooling had a rocky start with a brief placement in a special education classroom, but thanks to your parents, you made a comeback. Teaching is a noble profession, not something to be "entered into lightly." Now you are driven to teach and nothing else will suffice. I will be happy to share some of my experiences with you, and I hope that they will be useful to you as you begin this very honorable profession.

Laws and Policy Changes

As a special education teacher, you are coming into the profession at the perfect time! The Education of All Handicapped Children Act (1975) has just passed. You are in for the time of your life! You have been hired as the teacher of a self-contained special education classroom. Your students have intellectual disabilities (known to you as mild retardation). You have barely set up your classroom when an administrator waltzes in and says that you must do something that you have never done before. Furthermore, you must do something that no one else in the school district has ever done before . . . write IEPs. Ms. Rightslaw hands you a stack of 8 1/2" × 14" paper and strolls back out of the classroom. You look down at the paper and the only thing you see are: name, date, classification, and a lot of empty boxes waiting to be filled in by you. OMG!

This can happen to any teacher . . . An unexpected requirement, new laws and regulations, and so forth. Remain calm. Find out whatever you can about the new law or policy. (In the future, there will be something called the Internet where you will be able to locate a vast amount of information.) Don't be afraid to ask for help. Locate a teacher in your school or someone in the school district who can assist you. Collaborating with other teachers can be quite productive. And if anything goes wrong, you can make the revisions together. Hopefully, the school district will offer staff development sessions and workshops to address new policies and programs.

Organization and Classroom Management

Organization is very important for teachers; you will have so many responsibilities. First, let's talk about logistics. You have your new apartment, and you have your transportation (a cool Mustang). Your parents have taken you shopping to purchase "a teacher's wardrobe." One morning you receive a phone call, and when you answer it, your principal says, "Miss Hapless Novice, are you coming to work today? Your students are in the classroom waiting for you." You roll out of bed and arrive at work in a frazzled state. Don't forget to set the alarm clock.

You have a lot to remember . . . parent conferences, IEP meetings, interim reports, report cards, and so forth. You can stop writing on your hands and invest in a three-ring binder. You can use the binder to hold student progress data and an appointment calendar. Sticky notes are also very handy; you can stick them on the outside of the notebook or on your desk. (In the future, there will be handy tablets, smartphones, and smartwatches with audio reminders. You will be able to download apps that will aid you in your organizing efforts. Amazing!)

You told me that there is a teacher across the hall from you who has a very lively classroom. You say that students are climbing in and out of the windows? There is a girl washing her hair in the sink?! Now your students are getting a little antsy, and you are concerned about maintaining order in *your* classroom. You should have a classroom management plan and a behavior management system ready on the first day of school.

The classroom management plan should include a behavior management system. Your plan should discuss classroom procedures regarding out-of-seat behavior, going to the restroom, putting away materials, dismissal from class, and so forth. Your classroom management plan should be proactive and preventative. Arrange your classroom furniture and equipment in a way that will be most conducive to learning (and behaving appropriately). I am going to spend some time on this because you will not be able to teach in a chaotic environment, and your students will not get what they need—a good education. Remember to share your classroom management plan and behavior management system with administrators and parents because you want them to be supportive; they are a part of the team. Your behavior management plan should include three to five rules of behavior that you must have in order for you to teach. Your rules should target safety, respect, and responsibility. Establish a positive climate in your classroom. You may use rules such as:

- Be in your seat when the bell rings.
- Enter the classroom quietly.
- Raise your hand and wait for permission to____.
- Make positive comments.

You will need some consequences and some rewards to implement your behavior management system effectively. Spend some time discussing and explaining your classroom rules and expectations with your students. Be firm and consistent with the implementation of your behavior management system. Note: please do not include rewards and consequences that cannot be implemented. This would include consequences such as: No lunch for a month! I will never let you go to the restroom again! You will sit in the hall for the rest of the year! I will give you $500 if you will just stay in your seat!

Treat all students with dignity and respect. Never humiliate or embarrass a student. I know that you are working with students who have special needs. Some people think that people with special needs do not have feelings or that they do not know when they are being disrespected. Remember, you need to model the behavior that you are requiring of your students. Get to know your students as individuals; Find out about their families, what they like to do, and what activities they are involved in outside of school. Maybe you can attend a ballgame or dance recital. Attending these activities will demonstrate your concern for the students beyond the classroom environment.

Planning and Instruction

Planning and instruction is the heart of what we do as teachers. Most teachers have a planning period during the school day, and let me tell you, that will not be enough time for you to plan and prepare your lessons. As a novice, it will take you longer to prepare your lesson plans. You will need to spend some time after school in the classroom and/or at home preparing lessons. I prepare my lessons a week ahead; I use some time over the weekend to get this done. By planning and preparing, I mean reviewing all the content and gathering all the materials needed for the lessons.

You will be working with diverse groups of students over the years. Each student brings his or her own background knowledge and experiences to the classroom. Make your lessons engaging and interactive. Allow for movement and different ways for students to express their knowledge. They can draw, sing, write poems, dance, and so forth. I am a big fan of Universal Design for Learning (UDL); it is a proactive approach to instruction. Universal Design for Learning minimizes barriers and maximizes learning for *all* students. UDL is a teaching concept that I believe all teachers should embrace. Using UDL, a teacher can do three things: (1) Teach the information in different ways; (2) Allow students to show what they know in different ways; (3) Offer choices that engage students and maintain interest (CAST, Inc. 2012).

Be prepared to be flexible. Despite all your planning and preparation, ad hoc situations will occur and you may have to modify your plans. There will be unannounced fire drills, tornado drills, (Homeland Security drills). Your students may require more practice with the skills you are trying to teach. Be prepared to modify instruction and/or provide accommodations for students as needed.

Here are some one-liners for your consideration:

- *Laugh*—Remember to laugh. Sometimes that is all you can do, and it is very therapeutic.

- *Make time for your personal life*—Enjoy your family. Take care of yourself. Visit a spa regularly.

- *Don't sweat the small stuff*—Prioritize.

- *Love it or Leave it*—If your teaching situation becomes stale, try another setting, another subject, or another age group. Take a break. If none of these suggestions works, it may be time for a career change. It will be better for the children who would be in your classroom. They don't need the negative energy.

- *Communication*—Include the parents; communicate with them regularly. Send positive notes and postcards. (In the future, there will be email.)

- *Sit down sometimes*—Sit down and reflect on your practice. Are your students learning what was intended? Have you developed a positive relationship with your students? Can you explain your methodology? *Is* hindsight 20/20? Would you do anything differently? Why? How?

- *Don't stop believing*—You *can* make a wonderful difference in the lives of children!

Finally, continue your studies. Join and actively participate in professional organizations. There is so much to look forward to in the future—the age of technology. Technology and assistive technology are going to open so many doors for our students, especially students with special needs. There will be computers in the classrooms, in your office, in your home, and in your hands! Teaching is such an exciting field, and there is so much to learn. I have no doubt that you will be an exceptional teacher because you have such an indomitable spirit!

With kindest regards, I am

Yours Truly,
Dorea Bonneau

References/Resources

Center for Applied Special Technology (CAST) and National Center on Universal Design for Learning: http://www.udlcenter.org/aboutudl/take_a_tour_udl
Positive Behavioral Interventions and Supports (PBIS) www.pbis.org (developed by the U.S. Department of Education's Office of Special Education Programs)

¡Hola Mabel!

I have been thinking about you. Congratulations on completing your first year of teaching in Special Education! Making the decision to switch from teaching first grade to special education was not easy, but I am glad that you followed your inner call to help those students who need that extra support. Besides, you still get to work with students in primary grades, and I know how much you enjoy seeing their little eyes light up with every story, song, and experiment. I love the students' artwork and those cute bulletin boards!

This year was full of challenges: veteran peer teachers and administrators, academically and behaviorally challenged students, frustrated parents, and a low budget for curricular materials and traveling to conferences. Your peer teachers are very knowledgeable, and they are well liked and respected across the faculty and administration, so please do not hesitate to ask for help, and don't let yourself feel inadequate. Your fellow teachers are helpful and like to have fun in their classes! I know that often you tend to be shy and look for answers by yourself but, believe me, it would be much easier if you ask for help. They have been there, exactly where you are, not too long ago. In fact, they know your professors and graduated from the same teacher education program. Frequently you keep asking yourself, "Why are their classes so easy to teach? What am I doing wrong?" You should have no worries, believe me . . . Your classes will be like theirs soon! In fact, with time, your class will host many field experience students and interns and will be among the ones that professors continue to visit and recommend. Just be patient, ask for help, focus, and breathe! In addition, your school is lucky to have administrators who are very supportive and knowledgeable of the academic and behavioral needs of students with disabilities. They will continue to support your program and your decisions to include students in the general education classroom. I know that it is a challenge to mainstream students into general education classrooms, but your program is well liked within the school, and teachers will do their best to include your students in their classrooms. You will see how, through the years, more teachers will become more open to collaborate with your team!

The school district is negotiating a contract with behavior specialists who will be part of your team next year. Do not feel threatened . . . This will be very helpful. They will collect data that will help you make informed decisions about academic and behavioral goals for your students. It will also help to prepare better Individual Educational Plans (IEPs) that make more sense and would be easier to implement and to explain to parents. Another great asset will be such wonderful and kind teacher assistants. Your school will continue to employ caring and dedicated individuals who will become more than your peers—they will become family.

The students in your class present daily challenges that impact their academic success. Living in poverty and extreme family situations, school is about the only safe place for the majority of them. Some of your students live with grandparents or relatives in public housing and do not have family transportation; consequently, they do not experience recreational activities after school nor during the weekends. Therefore, keep looking for those resources within the community, as well as interesting places for field trips and guest speakers that will enhance their learning skills. You are lucky to live in such great college town that offers helpful resources. Kudos on your Chinese unit! The students truly enjoyed visiting the Chinese restaurant and the origami lesson from the owner last February. It is so hard to believe that for many students, the meals provided at school are often their only ones. Furthermore, some of your students do not have access to proper medical care, so, frequently, they come to school with colds and other illnesses. Please take care of yourself, wash your hands, drink water, and eat well!

Technology will be a wonderful asset in your classroom. The Apple computer that you had this year played only some games and served as a reinforcer for when the students finished their work early, but you will see how more advanced computers will make a world of difference soon. You will be able to have students collaborate on projects and even conduct their own research! I know that, at this point, you are wondering if you would really need to invest in a home computer. Oh Lord, please do! You will have access to so many helpful resources! Computers will change the world so much. Guess what? You will be able to show pictures of remote places, have pen-pals in classrooms from other countries and even chat! And do not even get me started with mobile phones. You will ask yourself how you made it without them!

Talking about your great future brings a major suggestion: Enjoy these coming years in your classroom. They will be precious and full of meaningful times. Your students and their families, although challenging at times, will bring wonderful memories and will prepare you for—guess what?!?!—going back to college for your doctoral program! I know that it is hard to believe, but there will be a time in which this dream will become a reality, and you will find a great opportunity to pursue a final degree. Yes, just like your parents and grandparents always suggested. After completing it, you will truly enjoy preparing other teachers, participating in wonderful professional development projects, and sharing that saying from the speaker that you heard last week in a conference: "Don't count your days . . . Make your days count!"

Have a great summer and wonderful 1990–91 school year!

Sincerely,
You, writing from the future,
Mabel O. Rivera, PhD
(Future university professor and president-elect of a state professional organization)

Dear Dreamer,

I have not thought about you much lately; worse even, I have never written you a letter. Do you think you would have read such a letter from an old woman on another continent? You might have dismissed it thinking that what separates us is so unbridgeable that it is not worthy of attention. You were a young psychology graduate in Bucharest, Romania, and this letter would have come from North Carolina, in the United States of America. What can unite us? What makes this letter valuable? What gives it weight over continents and time? The answer is that there are some overarching beliefs and values that united us in the end. Let me share some of what happened to you—to us—during these intervening years, and allow me to share with you some key insights your future self has gained.

What did you think you would do with a degree in psychology? Teach a classroom of children with disabilities? Not at all! You embraced clinical psychology because your father was a psychiatrist and because he was fascinated by psychology and human nature in general. He was an introvert, reading all the time and taking walks to think about what he read. He was the one who put a book in your hands one day and explained to you what intelligence testing means and how it was supposed to work. For every person we met, he was the one who always found interesting things to say and wonder about.

It's 1977 in communist Romania, and you just got a degree in clinical psychology, and you were dreaming that you would be able to find a job as child psychologist in a clinic or children's hospital in your home town, the capital city of Bucharest. What you did not know was that you were the last class to finish with such a degree. The dictator, Ceausescu, hated psychology (because it provides understanding of and can influence the human mind), sociology (because it shows the dynamics and functions of small and large groups of people), and philosophy (probably because he could not understand it), and, as a result, he decided that Romania should end studying and conferring degrees in these disciplines. Something had to be done with all the graduates of that year, so it was decided that they would be required to spend at least a year teaching in rural elementary schools. Psychology graduates were required to teach in special schools where all students had disabilities, mostly mild mental retardation.

So here you are, the week before the school starts, as a first grade teacher in a school for "mentally deficient children" in a small town in Romania. You did not have any training in pedagogy. All you knew were the main characteristics of children with mental retardation and how to conduct psychological testing. You did not even have any idea if there were books you could consult regarding what to do in the classroom. The first day of school, you were presented with a class of 15 children and the principal said to you, "By the way, we selected all the lowest functioning children from all the other three first-grade classrooms and put them in your class because I think it is easier to teach by ability level." You did not believe what he said because it was apparent to you that this was done in order to make the other teachers' lives easier and yours harder, since you had to implement the same curriculum with a very different group of children. Who were you to them? An intruder, someone outside the community, a young graduate who used to live in a big city who took this job only because she had to, and who will most certainly leave it as soon as she can.

You started quite optimistic, remember? You got the lesson plans done the best you knew how, and you tried everything you could to teach those kids. You tried different materials, different activities. Nothing seemed to work. The students were not retaining information, they were not paying attention, and they were talking and moving all the time. How were you supposed to teach them the letters of the alphabet? How were you supposed to teach them to read simple words and do basic additions, as was required by the curriculum? You felt that you should teach them other things, that you should have different activities for them, that they should not be required to sit at their desks all day. Your instincts told you that you needed to know more about their life at home, about their interests and experiences when they were not in the classroom. But that was not in the curriculum, and maybe there was something you missed by not being specifically trained to teach in the classroom. You sent notes home, and you had meetings with the parents, because you thought maybe they were not aware of their children's homework. While you were asking yourself what to do, something strange happened. A few parents began bringing meat, produce, and eggs to you while asking you to please not let their child repeat the grade. Surprised, you started researching the school policy and your colleagues' knowledge and expectations about the low-functioning children in your classroom. That's when you realized that the children to whom you were supposed to teach the alphabet were not likely to graduate from any school. Under other circumstances, they would have been rejected even from this special school, ending up usually in an institution or at home with their family during their entire adulthood. But you were the new teacher, and you were not one of the community, so there you go, trying to do the impossible with no preparation or experience.

Once you understood the situation, I wish you would have acted differently. I wish you would have done what would have been probably the best thing that happened to those kids that year. You could have started to play with them in the classroom. You could have understood that you did not need to teach these children a curriculum that was not suited to their learning needs. Nobody was evaluating you as a teacher. Nobody was visiting your classroom. You could have done whatever you wanted to make their school experience enjoyable and useful. They could have been on the floor matching puzzles instead of being seated behind their desks. Instead of being forced to remember letters and numbers, they could have been coloring and painting. Instead of being isolated at their desks, they could have been participating in group games. You could have realized then that your students needed to not only enjoy themselves but also to learn. Not letters and digits, but skills—social skills and life skills. That was your moment, dearest Dreamer, when you could have realized that being a clinical psychologist was not as exciting as changing the lives of children with disabilities and of their families through education.

Something happened, though, at that time, that will make you pursue a career in special education. Something gave you a signal that you might devote your life to understanding and educating children with disabilities and to trying to develop partnerships with their families. You did not recognize it then, but that's when it happened. You will choose to be a special education teacher, and you will be good at it because you believe in having high expectations for all children, you believe in differentiation, and you believe in the valuable partnership with your students' families.

It will only be years later—after years of teaching and developing educational plans for children with developmental disabilities and autism and earning a PhD in special education—that you will understand that all families are trying to do the best for their children, but they do not always know what their children need most. At that time in Romania, what families were hoping for, was an education for their children (with disabilities or not), even if it was only at an elementary level. Now I can tell you that those children, who did not find any joy in performing tasks way beyond their capabilities that they could not complete successfully, were eager to play games and cooperate with others in projects designed especially for them, and in that, they were no different from any other child. They could have greatly benefitted from educational goals and objectives other than academic.

It was a harsh experience for you, but one from which you learned a lot. I want you to remember that it is important to follow your instinct as a teacher, even if it is not a well-defined path. You need to have self-confidence and trust your passion for teaching. You believe in helping all children because you wanted to be a child psychologist. You will soon find out that children with disabilities are among the most vulnerable citizens of the society, and you will be advocating three important principles until the end of your career:

- Children with disabilities have the same needs as other children, but the way they are satisfied is different;
- Inclusion is not hard to accomplish if you ensure access, participation, and supports;
- Families should always be partners in education and treated as equal by the teachers.

Go on, dear Dreamer, continue your chosen professional path. Put passion, dedication, and accuracy in your work, and you will become quite accomplished professionally. Remember to build a set of worthwhile values and stick with them. And never forget this very important thing: **Those who teach should never stop learning!**

Yours truly,
Your accomplished and self-confident future self, Irina
(Irina Falls)

Dear Beginning Teacher Sheresa,

Congratulations on choosing a noble profession in which you will be able to combine your love for children, your selfless spirit, and your motivation to contribute to a purpose higher than yourself! You may not know this yet, but being a special education teacher will be one of the most challenging and rewarding ventures of your life so far. Through some of the lessons I now know as an educator, I will give you some "food for thought," including *considering the context of children's lives*, *staying positive*, and *letting go of trying to be perfect*.

You may not understand the magnitude of the daily ***context of your students' lives.*** As a special educator in a rural area, you know that most of your students are living at or below the poverty line in a county with limited resources and few career prospects for their caregivers. While the home lives and surroundings of your students do not define them, you should realize how they can affect the ways they think, behave, and respond. Many of your students have not been farther away than the next county, let alone to other parts of the state or country. They may come to you with limited previous experiences and subpar early care and education. Get to know them and what they care about. Immerse yourself more into the community through local events and churches so you can learn to love them and their families. This will serve you well in supporting your ability to connect with them and teach them. Remember, they are children first, and be careful not to blame them for their current lives, but help them to overcome the obstacles in their way and encourage them to believe in themselves.

You will have days when you are so tired you cannot see straight and are discouraged by the enormity of your work—the paperwork, the fact that students are so behind academically, the referrals for special education in middle school. ***Stay positive!*** Many things are less than ideal in your current work. Yes, it would be great if the students arrived to you knowing more, if you were not made the head of the special education department at your school in your first year as a teacher, and if children were not being identified as in need of special education as late as 13 or 14 years old—all of which are out of your control, so let them go. These things should not deter you. Stay laser focused on the work at hand, without letting it consume you. Be sure to put time into yourself (exercise, leisure reading, etc.) so you can stay well and be able to do your job. Remember, you are here for a reason, and you will learn SO MUCH about being a teacher and yourself!

So far in life you have tended to take life too seriously. Right now, I beg you to *let go of trying to be perfect and have fun!* Sure, the work you are doing is serious—after all children's lives and futures are in your hands. This fact should not weigh you down; instead, allow it to motivate you to have fun with it! Connect with your students where they are, but also bring the outside world into your classroom. You do not yet realize the importance and power of play and fun—even for your older elementary students and middle schoolers! Focus less on the content and more on finding ways to have fun, and be consistent and firm, while also "teaching" and learning about yourself. What a challenging and pleasurable feat! Laugh each and every day with your students because there are so many things to be grateful for and enjoy in life. Spark their interest and thirst for knowledge and excellence. Every day can be an amazing encounter you will grab by the horns and savor!

You have an amazing opportunity to serve in many roles in the lives of children. May you rise to this challenge and not look back, learn from your mistakes, harness your talents, and live life to the fullest!

Sincerely,
Your (Slightly) Older Self,
Sheresa Blanchard

Dear José,

Please accept this letter as a gift to and from yourself. You might want to sit down before you begin to read these words, for in all likelihood, they might take you by surprise. José, remember when at the age of eight you wished for a guitar at Christmas? As you already know, it did come true. Well, that very wish also set into motion a series of events that generated positive effects and lead you to discover a lifelong passion for music. Believe me when I tell you that, in the future, you will be able to inspire and transform lives of thousands of children of all ages through song. Your life's purpose will be simple: *Enable students to discover their own voices through music.* You will achieve this purpose by becoming a music teacher. But before you embark on this noble quest—*TEACHING*—I would like to offer some simple words of advice that someday you might find useful.

Allow children to love their innate musical instrument—their individual voice.

Consider this delicate instrument like a diamond in the rough; it must be discovered, polished, and shared with everyone to appreciate its unique beauty. No matter where you teach, you will find children eager to make and enjoy music. Develop a children's choir and perform with instruments, soloists, guest artists, and with audiences. Tell your students that if you are able to speak, you are able to sing! I want to give you a heads up, there will be a person who questions the value of teaching children to use their head voice when singing. No worries— that same person will be the first to congratulate you after the elementary choir performs with the University Symphony Orchestra!

Music enables us to transcend conditions that limit our natural capacity to create.

After teaching elementary general music, you will have an opportunity to teach choirs at the high school level. There, you will realize the joys of teaching choral music to students with different musical abilities. As you begin this new job, I want you to remember that all students share a need for success and self-expression. One particular semester, you will have an unusual number of students with cerebral palsy join your choir in wheelchairs. They come to you because they want to share their love for singing and feel part of the school community—something they might not get to experience in self-contained classrooms. Do not judge what you hear when they first sing, as they will improve in time. By the way, that same year, your choirs will receive superior ratings, including the choir with six students with disabilities. Focus on their joy of singing and reflect on how far they have come in just one year!

Make a difference, one child at a time, and you will change the world.

Teachers have many realizations throughout their careers. José, although it will take you some time to figure out, you will eventually realize that teaching music in under-privileged settings is your true calling. Racial and socioeconomic differences in schools present unique challenges that are very difficult to address. You will find yourself in this situation, but you will quickly discover that music has the power to unite people of all backgrounds. One of your students with a heartbreaking family situation will be so motivated to perform in your advanced choir that he will do anything to raise his grades to stay in school and eventually graduate from high school.

If you can speak, you can SING!

As a music teacher you will soon need to develop two very important skills. The first skill is identifying your students' needs and abilities. This includes helping students to match pitch or choose an instrument, selecting appropriate literature for your beginning band/choir, or providing the necessary skills to help students to become independent musicians (music literacy). If you ever become impatient with your students' progress, or lack thereof, just remember the concept of successive approximations, and remember that, in music, process is more important than the product. The second skill is to provide students with opportunities that will allow them to reach attainable goals. Start by making beautiful music in rehearsals. Have students perform for each other, for parents, and in community events. Perform at district, state, and national music conferences. Heads up, your advanced choir will someday be invited to perform at Carnegie Hall!!!

José, there will come a time when you will be asked to reflect on your teaching career. It will not be easy for you, but in the middle of this process, you will come to a point when memories from thirty years of teaching children will rush in your mind all at once and will overwhelm you with emotions of joy, love, and gratitude. As you write about it, time will suddenly stop, and in a moment of silence, you will realize how fortunate you are for the opportunity to be a part of thousands of children's lives through music and for being able to share your knowledge and passion for a *gift* that passes from generation to generation. The gift was not what I was able to give my students, but *what music was able to do in their lives*.

Wishing you a lifetime of joy teaching students to sing and make music!

Yours truly,
JR (José Rivera)

"Body, Mind, Spirit, Voice: It takes the WHOLE PERSON to sing and rejoice!"

—Helen Kemp

http://bodymindspiritvoice.com/

AFTERWORD

MESSES, GUESSES, and SUCCESSES:
What Can Be Learned by Walking in These Shoes

A Summarizing Reflection on the Common Themes
and the Lessons Contained in the Letters

"Wisdom is not just knowing fundamental truths, if these are unconnected with the guidance of life or with a perspective on its meaning. If the deep truths physicists describe about the origin and functioning of the universe have little practical import and do not change our picture of the meaning of the universe and our place within it, then knowing them would not count as wisdom."

Robert Nozick (1938–2002), U.S. philosopher and educator, in "What is Wisdom and Why Do Philosophers Love It So?" The Examined Life, Simon and Schuster (1989).

"We learn wisdom from failure much more than from success. We often discover what will do, by finding out what will not do; and probably he who never made a mistake never made a discovery."

Samuel Smiles (1812–1904), Scottish author and government reformer, in Self-Help; with Illustrations of Character and Conduct (1859).

"Knowledge comes, but wisdom lingers."

Alfred Tennyson (1809–1892), English poet, in "Locksley Hall (Line 141)" Poems (1842).

In classrooms and schools, each day offers many opportunities for new, worthwhile learning—for teachers, support staff, and administrators, as well as for students. Educators who remain in the profession inevitably accumulate a great deal of wisdom, usually gained in small increments and acquired over an extended period of time. The path to this high level of professional knowledge and skills is not always straight, nor is it likely to be clear of stumbling blocks. Before reaching this destination, the educator must embark on a journey that involves at least some measure of trial and error—traveling down a number of circuitous trails and winding lanes—in the search of what works best for them and their students. Indeed, many new teachers get caught up in numerous *MESSES* and are forced to make an assortment of *GUESSES* before finally stumbling on hard-won *SUCCESSES*.

An accumulation of learning experiences counts for naught unless used—consciously and purposefully—to improve one's practice. Examining personal beliefs and assumptions about teaching and learning can reveal discrepancies between what one *believes* and what one *does*. The process of *aligning beliefs and actions* can serve as a catalyst for professional growth and as a beacon guiding the way to successful practice.

Furthermore, this growing expertise becomes even more valuable if it is shared with others. Regrettably, it often is kept locked within the individual teacher unless opportunities, whether planned or spontaneous, are provided to bring it forth. Conversations with colleagues, mentees, and student teachers about common concerns—teaching and learning, motivation, classroom management, student behavior—as well as situations that require one to "think on one's feet," often serve as triggers for eliciting these insights.

One of the best ways to tap into this wisdom and to preserve it is through written reflection. However, most writers can write more convincingly and more coherently if they know the intended audience is someone with whom they desire to share their innermost thoughts, beliefs, and values. Who better to share with than YOURSELF—and especially your eager, energetic *future self* or your naive, perhaps overly idealistic, *younger self*? Judging by the letters compiled in this book, writing to their future/former selves inspired these prospective/current educators and motivated them to look within and to draw forth a flood of ideas and insights worthy of sharing with the novice teachers they will be or that they once were.

Although each letter is a unique expression of the individual writer, there are several overarching themes that run throughout the entire set of letters. Stated as guiding principles, these are as follows:

1. **Find joy in your chosen profession.** Don't let little aggravations get you down. Keep focused on your goals and mission as a teacher. Let your passion show!

2. **Get to know your students well, both academically and personally.** Find out what makes them "tick," and use that information to plan learning experiences that are relevant to them and that will motivate them and keep them actively engaged.

3. **Let your students know that you care about them as individuals.** Develop a caring, supportive relationship with your students, and let them know that you are there to help them reach their dreams. Never expect anything less than a child's best.

4. **Truly believe that all students can learn, and work hard to make that happen.** Accept students as they are, and take them as far as you can. Help them to help themselves.

5. **Don't try to be a friend to your students.** Instead, take on the role of a trusted adult for your students. They need to know that you have things under control.

6. **Make parents your allies.** Invite them to work in partnership with you to create opportunities for success for their children. Listen to them. Keep them informed.

7. **Be acutely aware of the impact a teacher can have on a child.** Weigh your words carefully before speaking, and treat all students with respect.

8. **Seek out exemplary teachers.** Do not hesitate to ask questions or to solicit advice from your mentor, other successful teachers, or your principal. Avoid those with negative attitudes and eschew gossip.

9. **Never stop learning.** Pursue opportunities to grow continuously, both personally and professionally. Demonstrate to students your enthusiasm for learning by continuing your own education.

10. **Plan, plan, and plan some more.** Be well prepared for each day. Have more planned than you think you will need. Be ready to change your plans if circumstances warrant.

11. **Make learning fun!** Plan creative and motivating learning experiences for your students. Find joy in learning alongside your students.

12. **Take risks.** Be willing to step out of your comfort zone and try out new ideas. Expect that you will make mistakes. Reflect on your successes and failures, learn from them, and move on.

13. **Learn how to organize and manage your classroom well.** Skills in these critical areas can help you to create an environment that is conducive to learning and reduce issues related to student discipline.

14. **Persevere, especially when the going gets tough.** Understand that there will be challenging days; expect them, plan for them, and get through them. Maintain a positive attitude.

15. **Take care of yourself.** Find the time to nurture yourself, and remember to pace yourself. Find ways to manage the inevitable stress. Build a network of support with those who care about you and believe in you.

16. **Believe in yourself.** Have confidence in your own abilities and your capacity to become a successful teacher. Take pride in your growth and remember to celebrate your accomplishments, as well as those of your students.

Any educator will recognize the abundance of hard-won wisdom that is summarized in these guiding principles. These principles are ones that are worthy of being disseminated to all beginning teachers; indeed, they provide sage advice for even the most seasoned veterans!

A teacher affects eternity; he can never tell where his influence stops.

Henry Brooks Adams (1838–1918), U.S. historian, critic, and author, in *The Education of Henry Adams* (1919).

INDEX OF LETTER CONTRIBUTORS

This index lists the writers of the letters included in this book and the page number on which their letters begin.